Treasure of Ambedkar Series 06

States and Minorities

What are their Rights and How to Secure them in the Constitution of Free India

Treasure of Ambedkar Series 06

States and Minorities

What are their Rights and How to Secure them in the Constitution of Free India

Dr B.R. Ambedkar

KALPAZ

Treasure of Ambedkar Series 06

States and Minorities
What are their Rights and How to Secure them in the Constitution of Free India

ISBN: 978-93-5128-261-7

First Published 1947
Reprint **2017**, in India by
Kalpaz Publications
C-30, Satyawati Nagar,
Delhi – 110052
E-mail: kalpaz@hotmail.com
Ph.: 9212142040

Printed at: G. Print Process, Delhi

PREFACE

Soon after it became definite that the framing of the future Constitution of India was to be entrusted to a Constituent Assembly the Working Committee of the All-India Scheduled Castes Federation asked me to prepare a Memorandum on the Safeguards for the Scheduled Castes for being submitted to the Constituent Assembly on behalf of the Federation. I very gladly undertook the task. The results of my labour are contained in this brochure.

The Memorandum defines Fundamental Rights, Minority Rights and Safeguards for the Scheduled Castes. Those who hold the view that the Scheduled Castes are not a minority might say that in this matter I have gone beyond prescribed bounds. The view that the Scheduled Castes are not a minority is a new dispensation issued on behalf of the High and Mighty Hindu Majority which the Scheduled Castes are asked to submit to. The spokesmen of the Majority have not cared to define its scope and its meaning. Anyone with a fresh and free mind, reading it as a general proposition, would be justified in saying that it is capable of double interpretation. I interpret it to mean that the Scheduled Castes are more than a minority and that any protection given to the citizens and to the minorities will not be adequate for the Scheduled Castes. In other words, it means that their social, economic and educational condition is so much worse than that of the citizens and other minorities that in addition to protection they would get as citizens and as minorities the Scheduled Castes would require special safeguards against the tyranny and discrimination of the majority. The other interpretation is that the Scheduled Castes differ from a minority and therefore they are not entitled to the protection which can be claimed by a minority. This interpretation appears to be such unmitigated nonsense that no sane man need pay any attention to it. The Scheduled Castes must be excused if they ignore it. Those who accept my interpretation of the view that the Scheduled Castes are not a minority will, I am sure, agree with me that I am justified in demanding for the Scheduled Castes, all the benefit of the Fundamental Rights of citizens, all the benefit of the Provisions for the Protection of the minorities and in addition special Safeguards.

The Memorandum was intended to be submitted to the Constituent Assembly. There was no intention to issue it to the public. But my caste Hindu friends who have had the opportunity to read the typescript have pressed me to give it a wider circulation. Although it is meant for members of the Constituent Assembly, I do not see any breach of decorum in making it available to the general public. I have therefore agreed to fall in line with their wishes.

Instead of setting out my ideas in general terms, I have drafted the Memorandum in the form of Articles of the Constitution. I am sure that for the sake of giving point and precision this method will be found to be more helpful. For the benefit of the Working Committee of the Scheduled Castes Federation, I had prepared certain explanatory notes and other statistical material. As the notes and the statistical material are likely to be useful to the general reader, I have thought it better to print them along with the Memorandum rather than keep them back.

Among the many problems the Constituent Assembly has to face, there are two which are admittedly most difficult. One is the problem of the Minorities and the other is the problem of the Indian States. I have been a student of the problem of the Indian States and I hold some very definite and distinct views on the subject. It was my hope that the Constituent Assembly would elect me to the States Committee. Evidently, it has found men of superior calibre for the work. It may also be because I am one of those who are outside the tabernacle and therefore undesirable. I am not sorry to find myself left out. My only regret is that I have lost an opportunity to which I was looking forward for placing my views for the consideration of the Committee. I have therefore chosen to do the next best thing—namely, to incorporate them in this brochure along with the Rights of Citizens, of Minorities and of the Scheduled Castes so that a wider public may know what they are, may value them for what they are worth and may make such use of them as it may deem fit.

"RAJ GRAHA,"
DADAR, BOMBAY- 14 — B. R. AMBEDKAR.

15
—
3

TABLE OF CONTENTS

PAGE

1. Proposed Preamble to the Constitution of the United States of India 3

2. Proposed Article I of the Constitution relating to the admission of Indian States and new territories into the Union 5

3. Proposed Article II of the Constitution containing Fundamental Rights for Citizens, Provisions for the Protection of Minorities and Safeguards for the Scheduled Castes 9

4. *Appendices*—

   I. Explanatory Notes on Preamble and on Articles I and II 27

   II. Text of the Poona Pact 54

   III. Disadvantages of the Poona Pact . . . 56

   IV. Statistics of Population 77

CONSTITUTION OF THE UNITED STATES OF INDIA

Proposed Preamble

We the people of the territories of British India distributed into administrative units called Provinces and Centrally Administered Areas and of the territories of the Indian States with a view to form a more perfect union of these territories do—

(For explanation, see page 27.)

ordain that the Provinces and the Centrally Administered Areas (to be hereafter designated as States) and the Indian States shall be joined together into a Body Politic for Legislative, Executive and Administrative purposes under the style *The United States of India* and that the union so formed shall be indissoluble

and that with a view :

(i) to secure the blessings both of self-government and good government throughout the United States of India to ourselves and to our posterity,

(ii) to maintain the right of every subject to life, liberty and pursuit of happiness and to free speech and free exercise of religion,

(iii) to remove social, political and economic inequality by providing better opportunities to the submerged classes,

(iv) to make it possible for every subject to enjoy freedom from want and freedom from fear,and

(v) to provide against internal disorder and external aggression,

establish this Constitution for the United States of India.

Proposed Article I

DETAILED ANALYSIS

Article I, Section I—*Admission of Indian States into the Union :*

Clause 1. Qualified Indian States and their admission into the Union.

Clause 2. Relation of Qualified Indian States which have not entered the Union and of the Disqualified Indian States to the United States of India.

Clause 3. Power of the United States of India to re-organize the territory of the Disqualified Indian States into suitable Administrative Units with a view to qualify them for admission into the Union as States of the Union.

Clause 4. Formation of new States within the Union.

Article I, Section II—*United States of India and New Territory :*

Clause 1. Incorporation of Foreign States into the Union.

Clause 2. Acquisition of new territory by the United States of India and its retention as unincorporated territory of the Union.

Article I—Section I

ADMISSION OF INDIAN STATES INTO THE UNION

Clause 1

The United States of India may, on application and on fulfilment of the terms prescribed by an Enabling Act of the Union Legislature laying down the form of the Constitution admit an Indian State into the Union provided the Indian State seeking admission is a Qualified State.

(For explanation, see pages 27-28.)

For the purposes of this clause a list of Qualified Indian States shall be drawn up. A State shall not be deemed to be a Qualified State unless it is proved that it is of a standard size prescribed by the Union Legislature and is endowed with natural resources capable of supporting a descent standard of living for its people and can, by reason of its revenues and population function as an autonomous State, protect itself against external aggression, maintain Law and Order against internal disturbance and guarantee to its subjects minimum standards of administration and welfare which are expected from a modern State.

Clause 2

The territory of an Indian State which is a Qualified State but which has not entered the Union and the territory of the Indian States which are disqualified shall be treated as incorporated territories of the United States of India and shall at all times form integral parts thereof and shall be subject to such parts of the Constitution of the United States of India as may be prescribed by the Union Legislature.

Clause 3

The United States of India shall have power to reform, rearrange, redistribute and amalgamate the territories of Disqualified Indian States into suitable Administrative Units for admission into the Union as States of the Union.

Clause 4

After a State has been admitted into the Union as a State no new State shall be formed or created within its jurisdiction nor any new State shall be formed by the junction of two or more States or parts of States without the consent of the Legislatures of the States concerned as well as of the Union Legislature.

Article I—Section II

Clause 1

The United States of India may admit into the Union any territory which forms a natural part of India or which is on the border of India on terms and conditions mutually agreed upon. Provided that the terms shall not be inconsistent with the Constitution of the United States of India and the admission is recommended by the Legislatures of one half of the States comprising the United States of India in the form of a resolution.

Clause 2

The United States of India may acquire territory and may treat it as unincorporated territory. The provisions of the Constitution of the United States of India shall not apply to the unincorporated territory unless a provision to the contrary is made by the Legistature of the United States of India.

Proposed Article II

DETAILED ANALYSIS

Article II, Section I—*Fundamental Rights of Citizens.*

Article II, Section II—*Remedies against Invasion of Fundamental Rights :*

Clause 1. Judicial Protection.

Clause 2. Protection against Unequal Treatment.

Clause 3. Protection against Discrimination.

Clause 4. Protection against Economic Exploitation.

Article II, Section III—*Provisions for the Protection of Minorities :*

Clause 1. Protection against Communal Executive.

Clause 2. Protection against Social and Official Tyranny.

Clause 3. Protection against Social Boycott.

Clause 4. Authority and obligation of the Union and State Governments to spend money for public purposes including purposes beneficial to Minorities.

Article II, Section IV—*Safeguards for the Scheduled Castes.*

Part I. Guarantees.

Clause 1. Right to Representation in the Legislature and in the Local Bodies.

Clause 2. Right to Representation in the Executive.

Clause 3. Right to Representation in Services.

Part II. Special Responsibilities.

Clause 1. For Higher Education.

Clause 2. For Separate Settlements.

Part III. Sanction for Safeguards and Amendment of Safeguards :

Clause 1. Safeguards to be embodied in the Constitution.

Clause 2. Amendment of Safeguards.

Part IV. Protection of Scheduled Castes in Indian States.

Part V. Interpretation.

ARTICLE II—SECTION I

FUNDAMENTAL RIGHTS OF CITIZENS

The Constitution of the United States of India shall recognize the following as Fundamental Rights of citizenship:

Fundamental Rights. (For explanation, see page 28.)

1. All persons born or naturalized within its territories are citizens of the United States of India and of the State wherein they reside. Any privilege or disability arising out of rank, birth, person, family, religion or religious usage and custom is abolished.

2. No State shall make or enforce any law or custom which shall abridge the privileges or immunities of citizens; nor shall any State deprive any person of life, liberty and property without due process of law; nor deny to any person within its jurisdiction equal protection of law.

3. All citizens are equal before the law and possess equal civic rights. Any existing enactment, regulation, order, custom or interpretation of law by which any penalty, disadvantage or disability is imposed upon or any discrimination is made against any citizen shall, as from the day on which this Constitution comes into operation, cease to have any effect.

4. Whoever denies to any person, except for reasons by law applicable to persons of all classes and regardless of their social status, the full enjoyment of any of the accommodations, advantages, facilities, privileges of inns, educational institutions, roads, paths, streets, tanks, wells and other watering places, public conveyances on land, air or water, theatres or other places of public amusement, resort or convenience, whether they are dedicated to or maintained or licensed for the use of the public, shall be guilty of an offence.

5. All citizens shall have equal access to all institutions, conveniences and amenities maintained by or for the public.

6. No citizen shall be disqualified to hold any public office or exercise any trade or calling by reason of his or her religion, caste, creed, sex or social status.

7. (i) Every citizen has the right to reside in any part of India. No law shall be made abridging the right of a citizen to reside except for consideration of public order and morality.

(ii) Every citizen has the right to settle in any part of India, subject to the production of a certificate of citizenship from the State of his origin. The permission to settle shall not be refused or withdrawn except on grounds specified in sub-clause (iv) of this clause.

(iii) The State in which a citizen wishes to settle may not impose any special charge upon him in respect of such settlement other than the charge imposed upon its own inhabitants. The maximum fees chargeable in respect of permits for settlement shall be determined by laws made by the Union Legislature.

(iv) The permission to settle may be refused or withdrawn by a State from persons :—

(*a*) who have been habitual criminals ;

(*b*) whose intention to settle is to alter the communal balance of the State ;

(*c*) who cannot prove to the satisfaction of the State in which they wish to settle that they have an assured means of subsistence and who are likely to become or have become a permanent burden upon public charity ;

(*d*) whose State of origin refuses to provide adequate assistance for them when requested to do so.

(v) Permission to settle may be made conditional upon the applicant being capable of work and not having been a permanent charge upon public charity in the place of his origin, and able to give security against unemployment.

(vi) Every expulsion must be confirmed by the Union Government.

(vii) Union Legislature shall define the difference between settlement and residence and at the same time, prescribe regulations governing the political and civil rights of persons during their residence.

8. The Union Government shall guarantee protection against persecution of a community as well as against internal disorder or violence arising in any part of India.

9. Subjecting a person to forced labour or to involuntary servitude shall be an offence.

10. The right of the people to be secure in their persons, houses, papers and effects against unreasonable searches and seizures, shall not be violated, and no warrants shall issue, but upon probable cause, supported by oath or affirmation, and particularly describing the place to be searched, and the persons or things to be seized.

11. The right of a citizen to vote shall not be denied or abridged on any account other than immaturity, imprisonment and insanity.

12. No law shall be made abridging the freedom of Speech, of the Press, of Association and of Assembly except for consideration of public order and morality.

13. No Bill of attainder or *expost facto* law shall be passed.

14. The State shall guarantee to every Indian citizen liberty of conscience and the free exercise of his religion including the right to profess, to preach and to convert within limits compatible with public order and morality.

15. No person shall be compelled to become a member of any religious association, submit to any religious instruction or perform any act of religion. Subject to the foregoing provision, parents and guardians shall be entitled to determine the religious education of children up to the age of 16 years.

16. No person shall incur any penalties of any kind whatsoever by reason of his caste, creed or religion nor shall any person be permitted to refuse to fulfil any obligation of citizenship on the ground of caste, creed or religion.

17. The State shall not recognise any religion as State religion.

18. Persons following a religion shall be guaranteed freedom of association and shall have, if they so desire, the right to call upon the State to pass legislation in terms approved by them making them into a body corporate.

19. Every religious association shall be free to regulate and administer its affairs, within the limits of the laws applicable to all.

20. Religious associations shall be entitled to levy contributions on their members who are willing to pay them if their law of incorporation permits them to do so. No person may be compelled to pay taxes the proceeds of which are specifically appropriated for the use of any religious community of which he is not a member.

21. All offences under this section shall be deemed to be cognizable offences. The Union Legislature shall make laws to give effect to such provisions as require legislation for that purpose and to prescribe punishment for those acts which are declared to be offences.

Article II—Section II

REMEDIES AGAINST INVASION OF FUNDAMENTAL RIGHTS

The United States of India shall provide :

Clause 1

(1) That the Judicial Power of India shall be vested in a Supreme Court.

Judicial Protection against Executive Tyranny.
(For explanation, see page 28.)

(2) The Supreme Court shall have the power of superintendence over all other courts or officers exercising the powers of a Court, whether or not such courts or officers are subject to its appellate or revisional jurisdiction.

(3) The Supreme Court shall have the power on the application of an aggrieved party to issue what are called prerogative writs such as *Habeas Corpus, Quo Warranto Prohibition, Certiorari* and *Mandamus*, etc. For purposes of such writs the Supreme Court shall be a Court of general jurisdiction throughout India.

(4) The right to apply for a writ shall not be abridged or suspended unless when in cases of rebellion or invasion the public safety may require it.

Clause 2

Protection against Unequal Treatment.
(For explanation, see page 29.)

That the Authority of the Legislature and the Executive of the Union as well as of every State throughout India shall be subject to the following limitations :

It shall not be competent for any Legislature or Executive in India to pass a law or issue an order, rule or regulation so as to violate the following rights of the subjects of the State :

(1) to make and enforce contracts, to sue, be parties, and give evidence, to inherit, purchase, lease, sell, hold and convey real and personal property.

(2) to be eligible for entry into the civil and military employ and to all educational institutions except for such

conditions and limitations as may be necessary to provide for the due and adequate representation of all classes of the subjects of the State.

(3) to be entitled to the full and equal enjoyment of the accommodations, advantages, facilities, educational institutions, privileges of inns, rivers, streams, wells, tanks, roads, paths, streets, public conveyances on land, air and water, theatres and other places of public resort or amusement except for such conditions and limitations applicable alike to all subjects of every race, class, caste, colour or creed.

(4) to be deemed fit for and capable of sharing without distinction the benefits of any religious or charitable trust dedicated to or created, maintained or licensed for the general public or for persons of the same faith and religion.

(5) to claim full and equal benefit of all laws and proceedings for the security of persons and property as is enjoyed by other subjects regardless of any usage or custom or usage or custom based on religion and be subject to like punishment, pains and penalties and to none other.

Clause 3

Protection against Discrimination.

(For explanation, see page 30.)

(1) Discrimination against citizens by Government officers in Public administration or by private employers in factories and commercial concerns on the ground of race or creed or social status shall be treated as an offence. The jurisdiction to try such cases shall be vested in a Tribunal to be created for the purpose.

(2) The Union Legislature shall have the right as well as the obligation to give effect to this provision by appropriate legislation.

Clause 4

The United States of India shall declare as a part of the law of its constitution :

Protection against Economic Exploitation.

(For explanation, see pages 30-35.)

(1) That industries which are key industries or which may be declared to be key industries shall be owned and run by the State;

(2) That industries which are not key industries but which are basic industries shall be owned by the State and shall be run by the State or by Corporations established by the State ;

(3) That Insurance shall be a monopoly of the State and that the State shall compel every adult citizen to take out a life insurance policy commensurate with his wages as may be prescribed by the Legislature ;

(4) That agriculture shall be a State Industry ;

(5) That State shall acquire the subsisting rights in such industries, insurance and agricultural land held by private individuals, whether as owners, tenants or mortgagees and pay them compensation in the form of debenture equal to the value of his or her right in the land. Provided that in reckoning the value of land, plant or security no account shall be taken of any rise therein due to emergency, of any potential or unearned value or any value for compulsory acquisition ;

(6) The State shall determine how and when the debenture holder shall be entitled to claim cash payment ;

(7) The debenture shall be transferable and inheritable property but neither the debenture holder nor the transferee from the original holder nor his heir shall be entitled to claim the return of the land or interest in any industrial concern acquired by the State or be entitled to deal with it in any way ;

(8) The debenture-holder shall be entitled to interest on his debenture at such rate as may be defined by law, to be paid by the State in cash or in kind as the State may deem fit ;

(9) Agricultural industry shall be organized on the following basis :—

(i) The State shall divide the land acquired into farms of standard size and let out the farms for cultivation to residents of the village as tenants (made up of group of families) to cultivate on the following conditions :—

(*a*) The farm shall be cultivated as a collective farm ;

(*b*) The farm shall be cultivated in accordance with rules and directions issued by Government ;

(*c*) The tenants shall share among themselves in the manner prescribed the produce of the farm left after the payment of charges properly leviable on the farm ;

(ii) The land shall be let out to villagers without distinction of caste or creed and in such manner that there will be no landlord, no tenant and no landless labourer ;

(iii) It shall be the obligation of the State to finance the cultivation of the collective farms by the supply of water, draft animals, implements, manure, seeds, etc ;

(iv) The State shall be entitled to—

(*a*) to levy the following charges on the produce of the farm :—

(i) a portion for land revenue ;

(ii) a portion to pay the debenture-holders ; and

(iii) a portion to pay for the use of capital goods supplied ; and

(*b*) to prescribe penalties against tenants who break the conditions of tenancy or wilfully neglect to make the best use of the means of cultivation offered by the State or otherwise act prejudicially to the scheme of collective farming ;

(10) The scheme shall be brought into operation as early as possible but in no case shall the period extend beyond the tenth year from the date of the Constitution coming into operation.

Article II—Section III

PROVISIONS FOR THE PROTECTION OF MINORITIES

The Constitution of the United States of India shall provide :—

Clause 1

Protection against Communal Executive.
(For explanation, see pages 35-39.)

(1) That the Executive—Union or State—shall be non-Parliamentary in the sense that it shall not be removable before the term of the Legislature.

(2) Members of the Executive if they are not members of the Legislature shall have the right to sit in the Legislature, speak, vote and answer questions.

(3) The Prime Minister shall be elected by the whole House by single transferable vote.

(4) The representatives of the different minorities in the Cabinet shall be elected by members of each minority community in the Legislature by single transferable vote.

(5) The representatives of the majority community in the Executive shall be elected by the whole House by single transferable vote.

(6) A member of the Cabinet may resign his post on a censure motion or otherwise but shall not be liable to be removed except on impeachment by the House on the ground of corruption or treason.

Clause 2

Protection against Social and Official Tyranny.
(For explanation, see page 39.)

(1) That there shall be appointed an Officer to be called the Superintendent of Minority Affairs.

(2) His status shall be similar to that of the Auditor-General appointed under section 166 of the Government of India Act of 1935 and removable in like manner and on the like grounds as a Judge of the Supreme Court.

(3) It shall be the duty of the Superintendent to prepare an annual report on the treatment of minorities by the public, as well as by the Governments, Union and State and of any transgressions of safeguards or any miscarriage of justice due to communal bias by Governments or their Officers.

(4) The Annual Report of the Superintendent shall be placed on the Table of the Legislatures—Union and State, and the Governments—Union and State, shall be bound to provide time for the discussion of the Report.

Clause 3

Protection against Social Boycott.

(For explanation, see pages 39-42.)

That Social Boycott, Promoting or Instigating a Social Boycott or Threatening a Social Boycott as defined below shall be declared to be an offence.

(i) *Boycott Defined.*—A person shall be deemed to boycott another who—

(*a*) refuses to let or use or occupy any house or land, or to deal with, work for hire, or do business with another person, or to render to him or receive from him any service, or refuses to do any of the said things on the terms on which such things should commonly be done in the ordinary course of business, or

(*b*) abstains from such social, professional or business relations as he would, having regard to such existing customs in the community which are not inconsistent with any fundamental right or other rights of citizenship declared in the Constitution, ordinarily maintain with such person, or

(*c*) in any way injures, annoys or interferes with such other person in the exercise of his lawful rights.

(ii) *Offence of Boycotting.*—Whoever, in consequence of any person having done any act which he was legally entitled to do or of his having omitted to do any act which he was legally entitled to omit to do, or with intent to cause any person to do any act which he is not legally bound to do or to omit to do any act which he is legally entitled to do, or with intent to cause harm to such person in body, mind, reputation or property, or in his business or means of living, boycotts such person or any person in whom such person is interested, shall be guilty of offence of boycotting.

Provided that no offence shall be deemed to have been committed under this Section, if the Court is satisfied that the accused person has not acted at the instigation of or in collusion with any other person or in pursuance of any conspiracy or of any agreement or combination to boycott.

(iii) *Offence of Instigating or Promoting a Boycott.*—Whoever—

(*a*) publicly makes or publishes or circulates a proposal for, or

(*b*) makes, publishes or circulates any statement, rumour or report with intent to, or which he has reason to believe to be likely to cause, or

(*c*) in any other way instigates or promotes the boycotting of any person or class of persons, shall be guilty of the offence of instigating or promoting a boycott.

Explanation.—An offence under this clause shall be deemed to have been committed although the person affected or likely to be affected by any action of the nature referred to herein is not designated by name or class but only by his acting or abstaining from acting in some specified manner.

(iv) *Offence of Threatening a Boycott.*—Whoever, in consequence of any person having done any act which he was legally entitled to do or of his having omitted to do any act which he was legally entitled to omit to do, or with intent to cause any person to do any act which he is not legally bound to do, or to omit to do any act which he is legally entitled to do, threatens to cause such person or any person in whom such person is interested, to be boycotted shall be guilty of the offence threatening a boycott.

Exception.—It is not boycott—

(i) to do any act in furtherance of a *bona fide* labour dispute;

(ii) to do any act in the ordinary course of business competition.

(2) All these offences shall be deemed to be cognizable offences. The Union Legislature shall make laws prescribing punishment for these offences.

Clause 4

Power of Governments to spend money for any purposes connected with the Government of India including purposes beneficial to the Minorities.

(For explanation, see page 42.)

That the Power of the Central and Provincial Governments to make grants for any purpose, notwithstanding that the purpose is not one for which the Union or State Legislature as the case may be may make laws, shall not be abridged or taken away.

Article II—Section IV

SAFEGUARDS FOR THE SCHEDULED CASTES

Part I. Guarantees.

Right to Representation in the Legislature.
(For explanation, see pages 42-48.)

The Constitution of the United States of India shall guarantee to the Scheduled Castes the following Rights :—

Clause 1

Right to Representation in the Legislature.

(1) *Quantum of Representation.*—(*a*) (i) The Scheduled Castes shall have minimum representation in the Legislature —Union and State—and if there be a group Constitution then in the group Legislature equal to the ratio of their population to the total population. Provided that no other minority is allowed to claim more representation than what is due to it on the basis of its population.

(ii) The Scheduled Castes of Sind and N.W.F. Provinces shall be given their due share of representation.

(iii) Weightage where it becomes necessary to reduce a huge communal majority to reasonable dimensions shall come out of the share of the majority. In no case shall it be at the cost of another minority community.

(iv) Weightage carved out from the share of majority shall not be assigned to one community only. But the same shall be divided among all minority communities equally or in inverse proportion to their

(1) economic position,

(2) social status, and

(3) educational advance.

(*b*) There should be no representation to special interests. But if the same is allowed it must be taken out of the share of representation given to that community to which the special interest belongs.

(2) *Method of Election—*

(*A*) *For Legislative Bodies.*

(*a*) The system of election introduced by the Poona Pact shall be abolished.

(*b*) In its place, the system of *Separate Electorates* shall be substituted.

(*c*) Franchise shall be adult franchise.

(*d*) The system of voting shall be cumulative.

(*B*) *For Local Bodies.*

The principles for determining the quantum of representation and the method of election for Municipalities and Local Boards shall be the same as that adopted for the Union and State Legislatures.

Clause 2

Right to Representation in the Executive.

Right to Representation in the Executive.
(For explanation, see pages 48-49.)

(1) The Scheduled Castes shall have minimum representation in the Executive—Union and State—and if there be a group Constitution then in the group Executive equal to the ratio of their population to the total population. Provided that no minority community is allowed to claim more than its population ratio.

(2) Weightage where it becomes necessary to reduce a huge majority to reasonable dimensions shall come out of the share of the majority community. In no case shall it be at the cost of another minority community.

(3) Weightage carved out from the share of the majority shall not be assigned to one community only. But the same shall be divided among all minorities equally or in inverse proportion to:

(i) their economic position,

(ii) social status, and

(iii) educational advance.

Clause 3

Right to Representation in the Services.

Right to Representation in Services.

(For explanation, see page 49.)

(*a*) The quantum of representation of the Scheduled Castes in the Services shall be as follows :—

(i) *In the Union Services.*—In proportion to the ratio of their population to the total population in India or British India as the case may be.

(ii) *In the State and Group Services.*—In proportion to their population in the State or Union.

(iii) *In the Municipal and Local Board Services.*—In proportion to their population in the Municipal and Local Boards areas.

Provided that no minority community is allowed to claim more than its population ratio of representation in the services.

(*b*) Their right to representation in the Services shall not be curtailed except by conditions relating to minimum qualifications, education, age, etc.

(*c*) The conditions prescribed for entry in Services shall not abrogate any of the concessions given to the Scheduled Castes by the Government of India in their Resolutions of 1942 and 1945.

(*d*) The method of filling up the vacancies shall conform to the rules prescribed in the Government of India Resolutions of 1942 and 1946.

(*e*) On every Public Services Commission or a Committee constituted for filling vacancies, the Scheduled Castes shall have at least one representative.

Part II. Special Responsibilities.

Provision for Higher Education.

(For explanation, see page 49.)

That the United States of India shall undertake the following special responsibilities for the betterment of the Scheduled Castes :—

Clause 1

(1) Governments—Union and State—shall be required to assume financial responsibility for the higher education of the Scheduled Castes and shall be required to make adequate provisions in their budgets. Such provisions shall form the first charge on the Education Budget of the Union and State Government.

(2) The responsibility for finding money for secondary and college education of the Scheduled Castes in India shall be upon the State Governments and the different States shall make a provision in their annual budgets for the said purpose in proportion to the population of the Scheduled Castes to the total budget of the States.

(3) The responsibility for finding money for foreign education of the Scheduled Castes shall be the responsibility of the Union Government and the Union Government shall make a provision of rupees ten lakhs per year in its annual budget in that behalf.

(4) These special grants shall be without prejudice to the right of the Scheduled Castes to share in the expenditure incurred by the State Government for the advancement of primary education for the people of the State.

Clause 2

Provision for New Settlements.

(For explanation, see pages 49-50.)

1. The following provision shall be made in the Constitution of the Union Government :—

(i) There shall be a Settlement Commission under the new Constitution to hold uncultivated lands belonging to the State in trust for settlement of the Scheduled Castes in separate villages.

(ii) The Union Government shall set apart annually a fund of Rs. 5 crores for the purpose of promoting the scheme of settlement.

(iii) That the Commission shall have the power to purchase any land offered for sale and use it for the said purpose.

2. The Union Government shall from time to time pass such legislation as may be necessary for the Commission to carry out its functions.

Part III. Sanction for Safeguards and Amendment of Safeguards.

Clause 1

The Constitution of the United States shall provide that—

Sanction for Safeguards. (For explanation, see pages 50-52.)

The United States of India undertakes to give the safeguards contained in Article II Section IV a place in the Constitution and make them a part of the Constitutional Law of India.

Clause 2

Mode of Amendment of Safeguards. (For explanation, see page 52.)

The provisions for the Scheduled Castes shall not be altered, amended or abrogated except in the following manner :—

Any amendment or abrogation of Section IV of Article II or any part thereof relating to the Scheduled Castes shall only be made by a resolution passed in the manner prescribed below by the more Popular Chamber of the Union Legislature.

(i) Any proposal for amendment or abrogation shall be initiated in the form of a Resolution in the more Popular Chamber of the Union Legislature.

(ii) No such Resolution shall be moved—

(*a*) unless 25 years have elapsed after the Constitution has come into operation and has been worked; and

(*b*) unless six months' notice has been given to the House by the mover of his intention to move such a Resolution.

(iii) On the passing of such a Resolution, the Legislature shall be dissolved and a new election held.

(iv) The original Resolution in the form in which it was passed by the previous legislature shall be moved afresh in the same House of the newly elected Union Legislature.

(v) The Resolution shall not be deemed to have been carried unless it is passed by a majority of two-thirds of the members of the House and also two-thirds of members of the Scheduled Castes who have been returned through Separate Electorates.

Part IV. Protection of Scheduled Castes in the Indian States.

Safeguards for Scheduled Castes in Indian States. (For explanation, see page 52.)

The Constitution of the United States shall provide that the admission of the Indian States into the Union shall be subject to the following condition :—

> " All provisions relating to the Scheduled Castes contained in Section IV of Article II of the Constitution of the United States of India shall be extended to the Scheduled Castes in the Indian States. Such a provision in the Constitution of an Indian State shall be a condition precedent for its admission into the Union."

Part V. Interpretation.

Scheduled Castes a Minority (For Explanation, see page 53.)

I.—For the purposes of Article II the Scheduled Castes, as defined in the Government of India Scheduled Caste Order, 1936, issued under the Government of India Act, 1935, shall be deemed to be a minority.

Scheduled Castes and change of Domicile (For Explanation, see page 53.)

II.—For the purposes of Article II a Caste which is a Scheduled Caste in one State shall be treated as Scheduled Caste in all States of the Union.

Appendix I

EXPLANATORY NOTES

Preamble

The Preamble gives constitutional shape and form to the Resolution on objectives passed by the Constituent Assembly on Wednesday the 22nd January 1947.

Article I—Section I

Clauses 1—4

The admission of the six hundred and odd Indian States into the Union raises many difficult questions. The most difficult of them is the one which relates to their admission into the Union. Every Indian State is claiming to be a Sovereign State and is demanding to be admitted into the Union in its own right. The Indian States fall into different classes from the view of size, population, revenue and resources. It is obvious that every State admitted into the Union as a State must have the capacity to bear the burden of modern administration to maintain peace within its own borders and to possess the resources necessary for the economic advancement of its people. Otherwise, the United States of India is likely to be encumbered with a large number of weak States which, instead of being a help to the Central Government, will be a burden upon it. The Union Government with such small and weak States as its units will never be able to pull its full weight in an emergency. It is therefore obvious that it would be a grave danger to the future safety of India if every Indian State were admitted into the Union without any scrutiny of its capacity to bear the burden of modern administration and maintaining internal peace. To avoid this danger, the Article proceeds to divide the Indian States into two classes: (1) Qualified Indian States and (2) Unqualified Indian States. It proposes that a list of Qualified Indian States should be drawn up as a first step in the procedure to be followed for the admission of the Indian States into the Union. A Qualified Indian State will be admitted into the Union on an application for admission and the fulfilment of the provisions of the Enabling Act which the Union Legislature is authorized to pass for the purpose of requiring an appropriate form of internal Government set up within the State which will be in consonance to the principles underlying the Constitution of the United States of India. The territory in the occupation of the Unqualified

Indian States will be treated as the territory of the United States of India and will be reorganized into States of suitable sizes by the United States of India. In the meantime those who are rulers of the territory shall continue to administer the territory under the supervision of the United States of India. The Act also declares that the Indian territory whether in the occupation of British Indian Provinces or of the Indian States is one and integral and will be so even though an Indian State has not entered into the Union.

Clause 4 provides that once a State is admitted into the Union, its integrity shall be maintained and it shall not be liable to sub-division except in accordance with the provisions contained in the clause.

Article I—Section II

Clauses 1 and 2

Clause 1 permits the United States of India to incorporate States which are independent but which are on the border and which desire to join the Union.

Clause 2 enables the United States of India to acquire territory and to incorporate it or to treat it as separate territory.

Article II—Section I

The inclusion of Fundamental Rights in the Constitution requires no justification. The necessity of Fundamental Rights is recognized in all Constitutions old and new. The Fundamental Rights included in the Article are borrowed from the Constitutions of various countries particularly from those wherein the conditions are more or less analogous to those existing in India.

Article II—Section II

Clause 1

Rights are real only if they are accompanied by remedies. It is no use giving rights if the aggrieved person has no legal remedy to which he can resort when his rights are invaded. Consequently when the Constitution guarantees rights it also becomes necessary to make provision to prevent the Legislature and the Executive from overriding them. This function has been usually assigned to the judiciary and the courts have been made the special guardians of the rights guaranteed by the Constitution. The clause does no more than this. The clause proposes to give protection to the citizen against Executive tyranny by investing the Judiciary with certain powers of inquisition against the abuse of authority by the Executive. This power takes the form of issue of writs. The High Courts in India possess these powers under the Government of India and under their Letters Patent. These powers are however subject to two limitations. In the first place the powers given by the Letters Patent are available only to the High Courts in the Presidency Towns and not to all. Secondly these powers are subject to laws made by the Indian Legislature. Thirdly the powers given by the Government of India Act 1935 are restricted and may prove insufficient for the protection of the aggrieved person. The clause achieves two objectives: (1) to give the fullest power to the Judiciary to issue what under the English law are called Prerogative Writs and (2) to prevent the Legislature from curtailing these powers in any manner whatsoever.

Clause 2

It is difficult to expect that in a country like India where most persons are communally minded those in authority will give equal treatment to those who do not belong to their community. Unequal treatment has been the inescapable fate of the Untouchables in India. The following extract from the Proceedings of the Board of Revenue of the Government of Madras No. 723 dated 5th November, 1892, illustrates the sort of unequal treatment which is meted out to the Scheduled Castes by Hindu Officers. Says the report:

"134. There are forms of oppression only hitherto hinted at which must be at least cursorily mentioned. To punish disobedience of Pariahs, their masters—

(*a*) bring false cases in the village court or in the criminal courts;

(*b*) obtain, on application, from Government, waste lands lying all round the paracheri, so as to impound the Pariahs' cattle or obstruct the way to their temple;

(*c*) have mirasi names fraudulently entered in the Government account against the paracheri;

(*d*) pull down the huts and destroy the growth in the backyards;

(*e*) deny occupancy right in immemorial sub-tenancies;

(*f*) forcibly cut the Pariahs' crops, and on being resisted charge them with theft and rioting;

(*g*) under misrepresentations, get them to execute documents by which they are afterwards ruined;

(*h*) cut off the flow of water from their fields;

(*i*) without legal notice, have the property of sub-tenants attached for the landlords' arrears of revenue."

"135. It will be said there are civil and criminal courts for the redress of any of these injuries. There are the courts indeed; but India does not breed village Hampdens. One must have courage to go to the courts; money to employ legal knowledge, and meet legal expenses; and means to live during the case and the appeals. Further most cases depend upon the decision of the first court; and these courts are presided over by officials who are sometimes corrupt and who generally for other reasons, sympathize with the wealthy and landed classes to which they belong."

"136. The influence of these classes with the official world can hardly be exaggerated. It is extreme with natives and great even with Europeans. Every office, from the highest to the lowest, is stocked with their representatives, and there is no proposal affecting their interests but they can bring a score of influence to bear upon it in its course from inception to execution."

The Punjab Land Alienation Act is another illustration of unequal treatment of the Untouchables by the Legislature.

Many other minority communities may be suffering from similar treatment at the hands of the majority community. It is therefore necessary to have such a provision to ensure that all citizens shall have equal benefit of laws, rules and regulations.

The provisions of Clause 2 are borrowed from the Civil Rights Protection Acts, 1866, and of March 1st, 1875 passed by the Congress of the United States of America to protect the Negroes against unequal treatment.

Clause 3

Discrimination is another menace which must be guarded against if the fundamental rights are to be real rights. In a country like India where it is possible for discrimination to be practised on a vast scale and in a relentless manner Fundamental Rights can have no meaning. The remedy follows the lines adopted in the Bill which was recently introduced in the Congress of the U.S.A. the aim of which is to prevent discrimination being practised against the Negroes.

Clause 4

The main purpose behind the clause is to put an obligation on the State to plan the economic life of the people on lines which would lead to highest point of productivity without closing every avenue to private enterprise, and also provide for the equitable distribution of wealth. The plan set out in the clause proposes State ownership in agriculture with a collectivized method of cultivation and a modified form of State Socialism in the field of industry. It places squarely on the shoulders of the State the obligation to supply capital necessary for agriculture as well as for industry. Without the supply of capital by the State neither land nor industry can be made to yield better results. It also proposes to nationalize insurance with a double objective. Nationalized Insurance gives the individual greater security than a private Insurance Firm does in as much as it pledges the resources of the State as a security for the ultimate payment of his insurance money. It also gives the State the resources necessary for financing its economic planning in the absence of which it would have to resort to borrowing from the money market at a high rate of interest. State socialism is essential for the rapid industrialization of India. Private enterprize cannot do it and if it did it would produce those inequalities of wealth which private capitalism has produced in Europe and which should be a warning to Indians. Consolidation of holdings and tenancy legislation are worse than useless. They cannot bring about prosperity in agriculture. Neither consolidation nor tenancy Legislation can be of any help to the 60 millions of Untouchables who are just landless labourers. Neither consolidation nor tenancy legislation can solve their problem. Only collective farms on the lines set out in the proposal can help them. There is no expropriation of the interests concerned. Consequently there ought to be no objection to the proposal on that account.

The plan has two special features. One is that it proposes State Socialism in important fields of economic life. The second special feature of the plan is that it does not leave the establishment of State Socialism to the will of the Legislature. It establishes State Socialism by the Law of the Constitution and thus makes it unalterable by any act of the Legislature and the Executive.

Students of Constitutional Law will at once raise a protest. They are sure to ask: Does not the proposal go beyond the scope of the usual type of Fundamental Rights? My answer is that it does not. If it appears to go beyond it is only because the conception of Fundamental Rights on which such criticism is based is a narrow conception. One may go further and say that even from the narrow conception of the scope of the Constitutional Law as comprising no more than Fundamental Rights the proposal can find ample justification. For what is the purpose of prescribing by law the shape and form of the economic structure of society? The purpose is to protect the liberty of the individual from invasion by other individuals which is the object of enacting Fundamental Rights. The connection between individual liberty and the shape and form of the economic structure of society may not be apparent to every one. None the less the connection between the two is real. It will be apparent if the following considerations are borne in mind.

Political Democracy rests on four premises which may be set out in the following terms :—

(i) The individual is an end in himself.

(ii) That the individual has certain inalienable rights which must be guaranteed to him by the constitution.

(iii) That the individual shall not be required to relinquish any of his constitutional rights as a condition precedent to the receipt of a privilege.

(iv) That the State shall not delegate powers to private persons to govern others.

Any one who studies the working of the system of social economy based on private enterprise and pursuit of personal gain will realize how it undermines, if it does not actually violate, the last two premises on which Democracy rests. How many have to relinquish their constitutional rights in order to gain their living ? How many have to subject themselves to be governed by private employers ?

Ask those who are unemployed whether what are called Fundamental Rights are of any value to them. If a person who is unemployed is offered a choice between a job of some sort, with some sort of wages, with no fixed hours of labour and with an interdict on joining a union and the exercise of his right to freedom of speech, association, religion, etc., can there be any doubt as to what his choice will be. How can it be otherwise ? The fear of starvation, the fear of losing a house, the fear of losing savings if any, the fear of being compelled to take children away from school, the fear of having to be a burden on public charity, the fear of having to be burned or buried at public cost are factors too strong to permit a man to stand out for his fundamental rights. The unemployed are thus compelled to relinquish their fundamental rights for the sake of securing the privilege to work and to subsist.

What about those who are employed ? Constitutional Lawyers assume that the enactment of Fundamental Rights is enough to safeguard their liberty and that nothing more is called for. They argue that where the State refrains from intervention in private affairs —economic and social—the residue is liberty. What is necessary is to make the residue as large as possible and State intervention as small as possible. It is true that where the State refrains from intervention what remains is liberty. But this does not dispose of the matter. One more question remains to be answered. To whom and for whom is this liberty? Obviously this liberty is liberty to the landlords to increase rents, for capitalists to increase hours of work and reduce rate of wages. This must be so. It cannot be otherwise. For in an economic system employing armies of workers, producing goods *en masse* at regular intervals some one must make rules so that workers will work and the wheels of industry run on. If the State does not do it the private employer will. Life otherwise will become impossible. In other words what is called liberty from the control of the State is another name for the dictatorship of the private employer.

How to prevent such a thing happening? How to protect the unemployed as well as the employed from being cheated out of their Fundamental Rights to life, liberty and pursuit of happiness? The useful remedy adopted by Democratic countries is to *limit* the power of Government to impose arbitrary restraints in political domain and to *invoke* the ordinary power of the legislature to restrain the more powerful individual from imposing arbitrary restraints on the less powerful in the economic field. The inadequacy nay the futility of the plan has been well-established. The successful invocation by the less powerful of the authority of the Legislature is a doubtful proposition. Having regard to the fact that even under adult suffrage all Legislatures and Governments are controlled by the more powerful an appeal to the Legislature to intervene is a very precarious safeguard against the invasion of the liberty of the less powerful. The plan follows quite a different method. It seeks to limit not only the power of Government to impose arbitrary restraints but also of the more powerful individuals or to be more precise to eliminate the possibility of the more powerful having the power to impose arbitrary restraints on the less powerful by withdrawing from the control he has over the economic life of the people. There cannot be slightest doubt that of the two remedies against the invasion by the more powerful of the rights and liberties of the less powerful the one contained in the proposal is undoubtedly the more effective. Considered in the light of these observations the proposal is essentially a proposal for safeguarding the liberty of the individual. No Constitutional lawyer can therefore object to it on the ground that it goes beyond the usual scope of Constitutional law.

So far as the plan has been considered purely as a means of safeguarding individual liberty. But there is also another aspect of the plan which is worthy of note. It is an attempt to establish State Socialism without abrogating Parliamentary Democracy and without leaving its establishment to the will of a Parliamentary Democracy. Critics of State Socialism even its friends are bound to ask why make it a part of the constitutional law of the land? Why not leave it to the legislature to bring it into being by the ordinary process of law. The reason why it cannot be left to the ordinary law is not difficult to understand. One essential condition for the success of a planned economy is that it must not be liable to suspension or abandonment. It must be permanent. The question is how this permanence can be secured. Obviously it cannot be secured under the form of Government called Parliamentary Democracy. Under the system of Parliamentary Democracy the policy of the Legislature and of the Executive is the policy of the majority for the time being. Under the system of Parliamentary Democracy the majority in one election may be in favour of State Socialism in Industry and in Agriculture. At the next election the majority may be against it. The anti-State-Socialism majority will use its law-making power to undoing the work of the pro-State-Socialism majority and the pro-State-Socialism majority will use its law-making power to doing over again what has been undone by their opponents. Those who want the economic structure of society to be modelled on State-Socialism must realize that they cannot leave the fulfilment of so fundamental a purpose to the exigencies of ordinary law which simple majorities—whose political fortunes are never determined by rational causes—have a right to make and unmake. For these reasons Political Democracy seems to be unsuited for the purpose.

What is the alternative ? The alternative is Dictatorship. There is no doubt that Dictatorship can give the permanence which State Socialism requires as an essential condition for its fructification. There is however one fact against Dictatorship which must be faced. Those who believe in individual freedom strongly object to Dictatorship and insists upon Parliamentary Democracy as a proper form of Government for a Free Society. For they feel that freedom of the individual is possible only under Parliamentary Democracy and not under Dictatorship. Consequently those who want freedom are not prepared to give up Parliamentary Democracy as a form of Government. However much they may be anxious to have State Socialism they will not be ready to exchange Parliamentary Democracy for Dictatorship even though the gain by such an exchange is the achievement of State Socialism. The problem therefore is to have State Socialism without Dictatorship, to have State Socialism with Parliamentary Democracy. The way out seems to be to retain Parliamentary Democracy and to prescribe State Socialism by the law of the Constitution so that it will be beyond the reach of a Parliamentary majority to suspend, amend or abrogate it. It is only by this that one can achieve the triple object, namely, to establish Socialism, retain Parliamentary Democracy and avoid Dictatorship.

The proposal marks a departure from the existing Constitutions whose aim is merely to prescribe the form of the political structure of society leaving the economic structure untouched. The result is that the political structure is completely set at naught by the forces which emerge from the economic structure which is at variance with the Political structure. Those who want socialism with Parliamentary Democracy and without Dictatorship should welcome the proposal.

The soul of Democracy is the doctrine of one man, one value. Unfortunately, Democracy has attempted to give effect to this doctrine only so far as the political structure is concerned by adopting the rule of one man one vote which is supposed to translate into fact the doctrine of one man one value. It has left the economic structure to take the shape given to it by those who are in a position to mould it. This has happened because constitutional lawyers have been dominated by the antiquated conception that all that is necessary for a perfect constitution for Democracy was to frame a Constitutional Law which would make Government responsible to the people and to prevent tyranny of the people by the Government. Consequently almost all Laws of Constitution which relate to countries which are called Democratic stop with Adult Suffrage and Fundamental Right. They have never advanced to the conception that the Constitutional Law of Democracy must go beyond Adult Suffrage and Fundamental Rights. In other words, old time Constitutional Lawyers believed that the scope and function of Constitutional Law was to prescribe the shape and form of the political structure of society. They never realized that it was equally essential to prescribe the shape and form of the economic structure of society, if Democracy is to live up to its principle of one man, one value. Time has come to take a bold step and define both the economic structure as well as the political structure of society by the Law of the Constitution. All countries like India which are late-comers in the field of Constitution-making should not copy the faults of other countries. They should profit by the experience of their predecessors.

Article II—Section III

Clause 1

In the Government of India Acts of 1919 and 1935 the model that was adopted for framing the structure of the Executive in the Provinces and in the Centre was of the British type or what is called by Constitutional Lawyers Parliamentary Executive as opposed to the American type of Executive which in contradistinction of the British type is called Non-Parliamentary Executive. The question is whether the pattern for the Executive adopted in the two Acts should be retained or whether it should be abandoned and if so what model should be adopted in its place. Before giving final opinion on this issue it would be desirable to set out the special features of the British type of the Executive and the consequences that are likely to follow if it was applied to India.

The following may be taken to be the special features of the British or the Parliamentary Executive :—

(1) It gives a party which has secured a majority in the Legislature the right to form a Government.

(2) It gives the majority party the right to exclude from Government persons who do not belong to the Party.

(3) The Government so formed continues in office only so long as it can command a majority in the Legislature. If it ceases to command a majority it is bound to resign either in favour of another Government formed out of the existing Legislature or in favour of a new Government formed out of a newly elected Legislature.

As to the consequences that would follow if the British System was applied to India the situation can be summed up in the following propositions :—

(1) The British System of Government by a cabinet of the majority party rests on the premise that the majority is a political majority. In India the majority is a communal majority. No matter what social and political programme it may have the majority will retain its character of being a communal majority. Nothing can alter this fact. Given this fact it is clear that if the British system was copied it would result in permanently vesting Executive power in a communal majority.

(2) The British system of Government imposes no obligation upon the Majority Party to include in its cabinet the representatives of the Minority Party. If applied to India the consequence will be obvious. It would make the Majority Community a governing class and the minority community a subject race. It would mean that a communal majority will be free to run the administration according to its own ideas of what is good for the minorities. Such a state of affairs could not be called democracy. It will have to be called imperialism.

In the light of these consequences it is obvious that the introduction of the British type of the Executive will be full of menace to the life, liberty and pursuit of happiness of the minorities in general and of the Untouchables in particular.

The problem of the Untouchables is a formidable one for the Untouchables to face. The Untouchables are surrounded by a vast mass of Hindu population which is hostile to them and which is not ashamed of committing any inequity or atrocity against them. For a redress of these wrongs which are matters of daily occurrence, the Untouchables have to call in the aid of the administration. What is the character and composition of this administration? To be brief, the administration in India is completely in the hands of the Hindus. It is their monopoly. From top to bottom it is controlled by them. There is no Department which is not dominated by them. They dominate the Police, the Magistracy and the Revenue services, indeed any and every branch of the administration. The next point to remember is that the Hindus in the administration have the same positive anti-social and inimical attitude to the Untouchables which the Hindus outside the administration have. Their one aim is to discriminate against the Untouchables and to deny and deprive them not only of the benefits of law, but also of the protection of the law against tyranny and oppression. The result is that the Untouchables are placed between the Hindu population and the Hindu-ridden administration, the one committing wrongs against them and the other protecting the wrong-doer, instead of helping the victims.

Against this background, what can Swaraj mean to the Untouchables? It can only mean one thing, namely, that while to-day it is only the administration that is in the hands of the Hindus, under Swaraj the Legislature and Executive will also be in the hands of the Hindus. It goes without saying that such a Swaraj would aggravate the sufferings of the Untouchables. For, in addition to an hostile administration, there will be an indifferent Legislature and a callous Executive. The result will be that the administration unbridled in venom and in harshness, uncontrolled by the Legislature and the Executive, may pursue its policy of inequity towards the Untouchables without any curb. To put it differently, under Swaraj the Untouchables will have no way of escape from the destiny of degradation which Hindus and Hinduism have fixed for them.

These are special considerations against the introduction of the British System of Executive which have their origin in the interests of the minorities and the Scheduled Castes. But there is one general consideration which can be urged against the introduction of the British Cabinet System in India. The British Cabinet System has undoubtedly given the British people a very stable system of Government. Question is will it produce a stable Government in India? The chances are very slender. In view of the clashes of castes and creeds there is bound to be a plethora of parties and groups in the Legislature in India.

If this happens it is possible, nay certain, that under the system of Parliamentary Executive like the one that prevails in England under which the Executive is bound to resign upon an adverse vote in the Legislature, India may suffer from instability of the Executive. For it is the easiest thing for groups to align and realign themselves at frequent intervals and for petty purposes and bring about the downfall of Government. The present solidarity of what are called the Major Parties cannot be expected to continue. Indeed as soon as the Problem of the British in India is solved the cement that holds these parties together will fall away. Constant overthrow of Government is nothing short of anarchy. The present constitution has in it section 93 which provides a remedy against it. But section 93 would be out of place in the Constitution of a free India. Some substitute must therefore be found for section 93.

Taking all these considerations together there is no doubt that the British type of the Executive is entirely unsuited to India.

The form of the Executive proposed in the clause is intended to serve the following purposes :—

(i) To prevent the majority from forming a Government without giving any opportunity to the minorities to have a say in the matter.

(ii) To prevent the majority from having exclusive control over administration and thereby make the tyranny of the minority by the majority possible.

(iii) To prevent the inclusion by the Majority Party in the Executive representatives of the minorities who have no confidence of the minorities.

(iv) To provide a stable executive necessary for good and efficient administration.

The clause takes the American form of Executive as a model and adapts it to Indian conditions especially to the requirements of minorities. The form of the Executive suggested in the proposal cannot be objected to on the ground that it is against the principle of responsible government. Indians who are used to the English form of Executive forget that this is not the only form of democratic and responsible Government. The American form of Executive is an equally good type of democratic and responsible form of Government. There is also nothing objectionable in the proposal that a person should not be qualified to become a Minister merely because he is elected to the Legislature. The principle that a member of the Legislature before he is made a Minister should be chosen by his constituents was fully recognized by the British Constitution for over hundred years. A member of Parliament who was appointed a Minister had to submit himself for election before taking up his appointment. It was only lately given up. There ought therefore to be no objection to it on the ground that the proposals are not compatible with responsible Governments. The actual proposal is an improved edition of the American form of Government, for the reason that under it members of the Executive can sit in the Legislature and have a right to speak and answer questions.

Clause 2

The proposal cannot be controversial. The best remedy against tyranny and oppression by a majority against the minority is inquiry, publicity and discussion. This is what the safeguard provides for. A similar proposal was also recommended by the Sapru Committee.

Clause 3

Social boycott is always held over the heads of the Untouchables by the Caste Hindus as a sword of Democles. Only the Untouchables know what a terrible weapon it is in the hands of the Hindus. Its effects and forms are well described in the Report made by a Committee appointed by the Government of Bombay in 1928 to investigate the grievances of the Depressed Classes and from which the following extracts are made. It illuminates the situation in a manner so simple that everybody can understand what tyranny the Hindus are able practise upon the Untouchables. The Committee said :—

> " Although we have recommended various remedies to secure to the Depressed Classes their rights to all public utilities we fear that there will be difficulties in the way of their exercising them for a long time to come. The first difficulty is the fear of open violence against them by the orthodox classes. It must be noted that the Depressed Classes form a small minority in every village, oppose to which is a great majority of the orthodox who are bent on protecting their interests and dignity from any supposed invasion by the Depressed Classes at any cost. The danger of prosecution by the Police has put a limitation upon the use of violence by the orthodox classes and consequently such cases are rare.
>
> " The second difficulty arises from the economic position in which the Depressed Classes are found to-day. The Depressed Classes have no economic independence in most parts of the Presidency. Some cultivate the lands of the orthodox classes as their tenants at will. Others live on their earnings as farm labourers employed by the orthodox classes and the rest subsist on the food or grain given to them by the orthodox classes in

lieu of service rendered to them as village servants. We have heard of numerous instances where the orthodox classes have used their economic power as a weapon against those Depressed Classes in their villages, when the latter have dared to exercise their rights, and have evicted them from their land, and stopped their employment and discontinued their remuneration as village servants. This boycott is often planned on such an extensive scale as to include the prevention of the Depressed Classes from using the commonly used paths and the stoppage of sale of the necessaries of life by the village Bania. According to the evidence, sometimes small causes suffice for the proclamation of a social boycott against the Depressed Classes. Frequently it follows on the exercise by the Depressed Classes of their right to use the common well, but cases have been by no mean rare where a stringent boycott has been proclaimed simply because a Depressed Class man has put on the sacred thread, has bought a piece of land, has put on good clothes or ornaments, or has carried a marriage procession with a bridegroom on the horse through the Public street."

This was said in 1928. Lest it should be regarded as a phase which has now ended I reproduce below a copy of a petition by the Untouchables of the village Kheri Jessore in the Punjab addressed to the Deputy Commissioner of the Rohtak District in February 1947 and a copy of which was sent to me. It reads as follows:—

"From

The Scheduled Caste People (Chamars),

Village Kheri Jessore, Tehsil and District Rohtak.

To

The Deputy Commissioner,

Rohtak District, Rohtak.

Sir,

We, the following Scheduled Caste (Chamars) of the Village Kheri Jessore, beg to invite your kind attention to the hard plight, we are put to, due to the undue pressure and merciless treatment by the Caste Hindu Jats of this Village.

It was about four months back that the Jats of the Village assembled in the Chopal and told us to work in the fields on a wage in kind of one bundle of crops, containing only about one seer of grains per day per man instead of food at both times and a load of crops, and annas 8 in addition which we used to get before above announcement was made. As it was too little and insufficient to meet both ends, we refused to go to work. At this they were enraged and declared a Social Boycott on us. They made a rule that our cattle would not be allowed to graze in the jungle unless we would agree to pay a tax not leviable under Government for the animals, which they call as "Poochhi." They even do not allow our cattle to drink water in the village pool and have prevented the sweepers from cleaning the streets where we live so that heaps of dust and dirt are lying there which may cause some disease if left unattended to. We are forced to lead a shameful life and they are always ready to beat us and to tear down our honour by behaving indecently towards our wives, sisters and daughters. We are experiencing a lot of trouble of the worst type. While going to the school, the children were even beaten severely and in a merciless manner.

We submitted an application detailing the above facts to yourself, but we are sorry that no action has been taken as yet.

It is also for your kind consideration that the Inspector of Police and Tehsildar of Rohtak, whom we approached in this connection, made a careless investigation and in our opinion, no attention was paid to redress the difficulties of the poor and innocent persons.

We, therefore, request your good self to consider over the matter and make some arrangement to stop the merciless treatment and threats which the Jats give us in different ways. We have no other approach except to knock at your kind door and hope your honour will take immediate steps to enable us to lead an honourable and peaceful life which is humanity's birth-right.

We beg to remain,
Sir,
Your most obedient servants,
Scheduled Caste People (Chamars),
of Village Kheri Jessore,
Tehsil and District Rohtak.

Thumb Impressions.

x x x

Copy forwarded to the Hon'ble Dr. B. R. Ambedkar,

Western Court, New Delhi.

Received on 1st February 1947."

This shows that what was true in 1928 is true even to-day. What is true of Bombay is true of the whole of India. For evidence of the general use of boycott by the Hindus against the Untouchables one has only to refer to the events that occurred all over India in the last elections to the Provincial Legislatures. Only when boycott is made criminal will the Untouchables be free from being the slaves of the Hindus.

The weapon of boycott is nowadays used against other communities besides the Scheduled Castes. It is therefore in the interests of all minor communities to have this protection.

The provisions relating to boycott are taken bodily from the Burma Anti-Boycott Act, 1922.

Clause 4

Such a provision already exists in Section 150 of the Government of India Act, 1935.

Explanatory Notes on Article II—Section IV

Part I—Clause I

There is nothing new in this clause. The right to representation in the Legislature is conceded by the Poona Pact. The only points that require to be reconsidered relate to (1) Quantum of Representation, (2) Weightage and (3) The System of Electorates.

(*1*) *Quantum*

The quantum of representation allowed to the Scheduled Castes by the Poona Pact is set out in Clause I of the Pact. The proportion set out in the Pact was fixed out of the balance of seats which remained after (i) the share of the other communities had been taken out; (ii) after weightage to other communities had been allotted, and (iii) after seats had been allocated to special interests. This allotment of seats to the Scheduled Castes has resulted in great injustice. The loss due to seats taken out as weightage and seats given to special interests ought not to have been thrown upon the Scheduled Castes. The allotment of those seats had already been made by the Communal Award long before the Poona Pact. It was therefore not possible then to rectify this injustice.

(*2*) *Weightage*

There is another injustice from which the Scheduled Castes have been suffering. It relates to their right to a share in weightage.

As one can see the right to weightage has become a matter of double controversy. One controversy is between the majority and the minorities, the other is a matter of controversy between the different minorities.

The first controversy relates to the principle of weightage. The majority insists that the minority has no right to representation in excess of the ratio of its population to the total population. Why this rule is insisted upon by the majority it is difficult to understand. Is it because the majority wants to establish its own claim to population ratio so that it may always remain as a majority and act as a majority ? Or is it because of the fact that a minority no matter how much weightage was given to it must remain a minority and cannot alter the fact that the majority will always be able to impose its will upon it. The first ground leads to a complete negation of the basic conception of majority rule which if rightly understood means nothing more than a decision of the majority to which the minority has reconciled itself. This cannot be the intention of the Majority. One must put a more charitable construction and assume that the argument on which the contention of the majority rests is the second and not the first. That a minority even with weightage will remain a minority has to be accepted in view of the insistence of a Communal Majority to remain a majority and to claim the privileges of a political majority which it is not. But surely there is a difference between a defeat which is a complete rout and a defeat which is almost victory though not a victory. Cricketers know what difference there is between the defeat of a team by a few runs, a defeat by a few wickets and a defeat by one whole innings. The defeat by one whole innings is a complete frustration which a defeat by a few runs is not. Such a frustration when it comes about in the political life of a minority depresses and demoralizes and crushes the spirit of the minority. This must be avoided at any price. Looked at from this point of view there is no doubt that the rule of population—ratio—representation insisted upon by the majority is wrong. What a minority needs is not more representation but effective representation.

And what is effective representation? Obviously the effectiveness of representation depends upon its being large enough to give the minority the sense of not being entirely overwhelmed by the majority. Representation according to population to a minority or to the minorities combined may be effective by reason of the fact that the population of a minority where there is only one or of the combined minorities where there are many is large enough to secure effective minority representation. But there may be cases where the population of a minority or of the minorities combined is too small to secure such effective representation if the population ratio of a minority is taken as an inflexible standard to determine its quantum of representation. To insist upon such a standard is to make mockery of the protection to the minority which is the purpose behind the right to representation which is accepted as the legitimate claim of a minority. In such cases weightage which is another name for deduction from the quantum of representation which is due to the majority on the basis of its population becomes essential and the majority if it wishes to be fair and honest must concede it. There can therefore be no quarrel over the principle of weightage. On this footing the controversy becomes restricted to the question, how is the magnitude of weightage to be determined ? This obviously is a question of adjustment and not of principle.

There can therefore be no manner of objection to the principle of weightage. The demand for weightage is however a general demand of all the minorities and the Scheduled Castes must join them in it where the majority is too big. What is however wrong with the existing weightage is unequal distribution among the various minorities. At present, some minorities have secured a lion's share and some like the Untouchables have none. This wrong must be rectified by a distribution of the weightage on some intelligible principle.

(3) *Electorates*

1. The method of election to the seats allotted to the Scheduled Castes is set out in clauses (2) to (4) of the Poona Pact. It provides for two elections : (1) Primary election and (2) Final election. The Primary election is by a separate electorate, of the Scheduled Castes. It is only a qualifying election and determines who is entitled to stand in the final election on behalf of the Scheduled Castes for the seats reserved to them. The final election is by a joint electorate in which both caste Hindus and the Scheduled Castes can vote and the final result is determined by their joint vote.

2. Clause (5) of the Poona Pact has limited the system of Primary election to ten years which means that any election taking place after 1947 will be by a system of joint electorates and reserved seats pure and simple.

3. Even if the Hindus agreed to extend the system of double election for a further period it will not satisfy the Scheduled Castes. There are two objections to the retention of the Primary election. Firstly, it does not help the Scheduled Castes to elect a man who is their best choice. As will be seen from Appendix III, the Scheduled Caste candidate who tops the poll in the Primary election fails to succeed in the Final election and the Scheduled Caste candidate who fails in the Primary election tops the poll in the Final election. Secondly, the Primary election is for the most part a fiction and not a fact. In the last election, out of 151 seats reserved for the Scheduled Castes there were primary elections only in 43. This is because it is impossible

for the Scheduled Castes to bear the expenses of two elections—primary and final. To retain such a system is worse than useless.

4. Things will be much worse under the system of joint electorates and reserved seats which will hereafter become operative under the terms of the Poona Pact. This is no mere speculation. The last election has conclusively proved that the Scheduled Castes can be completely disfranchised in a joint electorate. As will be seen from the figures given in Appendix III, the Scheduled Caste candidates have not only been elected by Hindu votes when the intention was that they should be elected by Scheduled Caste votes but what is more the Hindus have elected those Scheduled Caste candidates who had failed in the Primary election. This is a complete disfranchisement of the Scheduled Castes. The main reason is to be found in the enormous disparity between the voting strength of the Scheduled Castes and the caste Hindus in most of the constituencies as may be seen from figures given in Appendix III. As the Simon Commission has observed, the device of the reserved seats ceases to be workable where the protected community constitutes an exceedingly small fraction of any manageable constituency. This is exactly the case of the Scheduled Castes. This disparity cannot be ignored. It will remain even under adult suffrage. That being the case, a fool-proof and a knave-proof method must be found to ensure real representation to the Scheduled Castes. Such a method must involve the abolition of—

(i) the Primary election as a needless and heavy encumbrance; and

(ii) the substitution of separate electorates.

5. One of the issues which has embittered the relations between the Hindus and the Scheduled Castes in the political field is the issue of electorates. The Scheduled Castes are insisting upon separate electorates. The Hindus are equally insistent on opposing the demand. To arrive at a settlement on this issue—without which there can be no peace and amity between the Hindus and the Scheduled Castes—it is necessary to determine who is right and who is wrong and whether the opposition is based on rational grounds or is based on mere prejudice.

6. The grounds which are generally urged against the demand of the Scheduled Castes for separate electorates are :—

(i) that the Scheduled Castes are not a minority;

(ii) that the Scheduled Castes are Hindus and therefore they cannot have separate electorates;

(iii) that separate electorates will perpetuate untouchability;

(iv) that separate electorates are anti-national; and

(v) that separate electorates enable British Imperialism to influence the communities having separate electorates to act against the interests of the country.

7. Are these arguments valid?

(i) To say that the Scheduled Castes are not a minority is to misunderstand the meaning of the word 'minority.' Separation in religion is not the only test of a minority. Nor is it a good and efficient test. Social discrimination constitutes the real test for determining whether a social group is or is not a minority. Even Mr. Gandhi thought it logical and practical to adopt this test in preference to that of religious separation. Following this test, Mr. Gandhi in an editorial under the heading "The Fiction of Majority" in the *Harijan* dated 21st October 1939 has given his opinion that the Scheduled Castes are the only real minority in India.

(ii) To argue that the Scheduled Castes are Hindus and therefore cannot demand separate electorates is to put the same argument in a different form. To make religious affiliation the determining factor for constitutional safeguards is to overlook the fact that the religious affiliation may be accompanied by an intense degree of social separation and discrimination. The belief that separate electorates go with separation in religion arises from the fact that those minorities who have been given separate electorates happen to be religious minorities. This, however, is not correct. Muslims are given separate electorates not because they are different from Hindus in point of religion. They are given separate electorates because—and this is the fundamental fact—the social relations between the Hindus and the Musalmans are marked by social discrimination. To put the point in a somewhat different manner, the nature of the electorates is determined not by reference to religion but by reference to social considerations. That it is social considerations and not religious affiliation or disaffiliation which is accepted as the basis of determining the nature of the electorates is best illustrated by the arrangements made under the Government of India Act (1935) for the Christian community in India. The Christian community is divided into three sections—Europeans, Anglo-Indians and Indian Christians. In spite of the fact that they all belong to the same religion each section has a separate electorate. This shows that what is decisive is not religious affiliation but social separation.

(iii) To urge that separate electorates prevent solidarity between the Untouchables and the Caste Hindus is the result of confused thinking. Elections take place once in five years. Assuming there were joint electorates, it is difficult to understand how social solidarity between the Hindus and the Untouchables can be promoted by their devoting one day for voting together when out of the rest of the five years they are leading severely separate lives ? Similarly, assuming that there were separate electorates it is difficult to understand how one day devoted to separate voting in the course of five years can make for greater separation than what already exists ? Or contrarywise, how can one day in five years devoted to separate voting prevent those who wish to work for their union from carrying out their purposes. To make it concrete, how can separate electorate for the Untouchables prevent intermarriage or interdining being introduced between them and the Hindus ? It is therefore futile to say that separate electorates for the Untouchables will perpetuate separation between them and the Hindus.

(iv) To insist that separate electorates create anti-national spirit is contrary to experience. The Sikhs have separate electorates. But no one can say that the Sikhs are anti-national. The Muslims have had separate electorates right from 1909. Mr. Jinnah had been elected by separate electorates. Yet, Mr. Jinnah was the apostle of Indian Nationalism up to 1935. The Indian Christians have separate electorates. Nonetheless a good lot of them have shown their partiality to the Congress if they have not been actually returned on the Congress ticket. Obviously, nationalism and anti-nationalism have nothing to do with the electoral system. They are the result of extra electoral forces.

(v) This agrument has no force. It is nothing but escapism. Be that as it may, with free India any objection to separate electorates on such a ground must vanish.

8. The reason why the arguments advanced by the opponents of separate electorates do not stand the scrutiny of logic and experience is due entirely to the fact that their approach to the subject is fundamentally wrong. It is wrong in two respects :—

(i) They fail to realize that the system of electorates has nothing to do with the religious nexus or communal nexus. It is nothing but a mechanism to enable a minority to return its true representative to the Legislature. Being a mechanism for the protection of a minority it follows that whether the electorate should be joint or separate must be left to be determined by the minority.

(ii) They fail to make any distinction between the demand for separate electorates by a majority community and a similar demand made by a minority community. A majority community has no right to demand separate electorates. The reason is simple. A right by a majority community to demand separate electorates is tantamount to a right to establish the Government of the majority community over the minority community without the consent of the minority. This is contrary to the well-established doctrine of democracy that government must be with the consent of the governed. No such evil consequence follows from the opposite principle namely that a minority community is entitled to determine the nature of the electorates suited to its interests, because there is no possibility of the minority being placed in a position to govern the majority.

9. A correct attitude towards the whole question rests on the following axioms :—

(i) The system of electorates being a devise for the protection of the minority, the issue whether the electoral system should be the joint electorate or separate electorate must be left to the wishes of the minority. If it is large enough to influence the majority it will choose joint electorates. If it is too small for the purpose, it will prefer separate electorates for fear of being submerged.

(ii) The majority, being in a position to rule can have no voice in the determination of the system of electorates. If the minority wants joint electorates, the majority must submit itself to joint electorates. If the minority decides to have separate electorates for itself the majority cannot refuse to grant them. In other words, the majority must look to the decision of the minority and abide by it.

Part I—Clause 2

This demand may appear to be outside the Poona Pact in as much as the Poona Pact made no provision for it. This would not be correct. As a matter of fact, if no provision was made, it was because there was no need to make such a provision. This was due to two reasons: *Firstly*, it was due to the fact that at the time when the Poona Pact was made no community was guaranteed by law a specific quantum of representation in the Executive, *Secondly*, the representation of the communities in the Executive was left to a convention which the Governor by his Instrument of Instructions was required to see observed. Experience has shown that the quantum of representation of the Scheduled Castes in the Executive should now be fixed.

Part I—Clause 3

This is not a new demand. Clause 8 of the Poona Pact guarantees to the Scheduled Castes fair representation in Public Services. It does not, however, define the quantum of representation. The demand has been admitted by the Government of India as legitimate and even the quantum of representation has been defined. All that remains is to give it a statutory basis.

Part II—Clause 1

This is not a new demand. Clause 9 of Poona Pact guarantees that an adequate sum shall be earmarked for the education of the Scheduled Castes. It does not define the quantum. All that the demand does is to define the quantum of liability the State should take. In this connection reference may be made to section 83 of the Government of India Act, 1935, which relates to the education of the Anglo-Indians and Europeans and to the grants made to the Aligarh and Benares Hindu Universities by the Central Government.

Part II—Clause 2

This is a new demand but is justified by circumstances. At present, the Hindus live in the village and the Untouchables live in the Ghettoes. The object is to free the Untouchables from the thraldom of the Hindus. So long as the present arrangement continues it is impossible for the Untouchables either to free themselves from the yoke of the Hindus or to get rid of their Untouchability. It is the close-knit association of the Untouchables with the Hindus living in the same villages which marks them out as Untouchables and which enables the Hindus to identify them as being Untouchables. India is admittedly a land of villages and so long as the village system provides an easy method of marking out and identifying the Untouchables, the Untouchable has no escape from Untouchability. It is the system of the Village plus the Ghetto which perpetuates Untouchability and the Untouchables therefore demand that the nexus should be broken and the Untouchables who are as a matter of fact socially separate should be made separate geographically and territorially also, and be settled into separate villages exclusively of Untouchables in which the distinction of the high and the low and of Touchable and Untouchable will find no place.

The second reason for demanding separate settlements arises out of the economic position of the Untouchables in the villages. That their condition is most pitiable no one will deny. They are a body of landless labourers who are entirely dependent upon such employment as the Hindus may choose to give them and on such wages as the Hindus may find it profitable to pay. In the villages in which they live they cannot engage in any trade or occupation, for owing to untouchability no Hindu will deal with them. It is therefore obvious that there is no way of earning a living which is open to the Untouchables so long as they live in a Ghetto as a dependent part of the Hindu Village.

This economic dependence has also other consequences besides the condition of poverty and degradation which proceeds from it. The Hindu has a Code of life, which is part of his religion. This Code of life gives him many privileges and heaps upon the Untouchable many indignities which are incompatible with the dignity and sanctity of human life. The Untouchables all over India are fighting against the indignities and injustices which the Hindus in the name of their religion have heaped upon them. A perpetual war is going on every day in every village between the Hindus and the Untouchables. It does not see the light of the day. The Hindu Press is not prepared to give it publicity lest it should injure the cause of their freedom in the eyes of the world. The existence of a grim struggle between the Touchables and the Untouchables is however a fact. Under the village system the Untouchable has found himself greatly handicapped in his struggle for free and honourable life. It is a contest between the Hindus who are economically and socially strong and the Untouchables who are economically poor and numerically small. That the Hindus most often succeed in suppressing the Untouchables is due to many causes. The Hindus have the Police and the Magistracy on their side. In a quarrel between the Untouchables and the Hindus the Untouchables will never get protection from the Police and justice from the Magistrate. The Police and the Magistracy naturally love their class more than their duty. But the chief weapon in the armoury of the Hindus is economic power which they possess over the poor Untouchables living in the village. The proposal may be dubbed escapism. But the only alternative is perpetual slavery.

Part III—Clause 1

No country which has the problem of Communal majority and Communal minority is without some kind of an arrangement whereby they agree to share political power. South Africa has such an understanding. So has Canada. The arrangement for sharing political power between the English and the French in Canada is carried to the minutes office. In referring to this fact Mr. Porritt in his book on the Evolution of the Dominion of Canada says :—

"Conditions at Ottawa, partly due to race and language, and partly to long-prevailing ideas as to the distribution of all government patronage, have militated against the Westminster precedent of continuing a member in the chair for two or three parliaments, regardless of the fortunes of political parties at general elections. There is a new speaker at Ottawa for each new House of Commons; and it has long been a custom that when one political party continues in power for two or three parliaments, if the speaker in one parliament is of British extraction the next one shall be a French-Canadian.

"It is a rule also that the offices of speaker and of deputy-speaker can at no time be held by men of the same race. If the speaker is a French-Canadian, the deputy-speaker, who is also chairman of committees, must be an English-speaking Canadian; for the rule of the House is that the member elected to serve as deputy-speaker shall be required to possess the full and practical knowledge of the language which is not that of the speaker for the time being.

"The clerkship and the assistant clerkship of the house, and the offices of sergeant-at-arms and deputy-sergeant-at-arms—all appointive as distinct from elective offices—are, by usage, also similarly divided between the two races.

"Nearly all the offices, important and unimportant, connected with parliament, with the Senate as well as with the House, are distributed in accordance with these rules or usages. A roll call of the staffs of the two houses, including even the boys in knicker-bockers who act as pages, would contain the names of almost as many French-Canadians as Canadians of British ancestry.

"The rules and usages by virtue of which this distribution of offices is made are older than Confederation. They date back to the early years of the United Provinces, when Quebec and Ontario elected exactly the same number of members to the legislature, and when these were the only provinces in the union.

"Quebec to-day elects only 65 of the 234 members of the House of Commons. Its population is not one-fourth of the population of the Dominion. Its contribution to Dominion revenues does not exceed one-sixth. But an equal division of the offices of the house of commons is regarded by Quebec as necessary to the preservation of its rights and privileges; and so long as each political party, when it is in power, is dependent on support from French-Canada, it will be nearly as difficult to ignore the claim of Quebec to these parliamentary honors and offices as it would be to repeal the clause in the British North America Act that safeguards the separate schools system."

Unfortunately for the minorities in India, Indian Nationalism has developed a new doctrine which may be called the Divine Right of the Majority to rule the minorities according to the wishes of the majority. Any claim for the sharing of power by the minority is called communalism while the monopolizing of the whole power by the majority is called Nationalism. Guided by such a political philosophy the majority is not prepared to allow the minorities to share political power nor is it willing to respect any convention made in that behalf as is evident from their repudiation of the obligation (to include representatives of the minorities in the cabinet) contained in the Instrument of Instructions issued to the Governors in the Government of India Act of 1935. Under these circumstances there is no way left but to have the rights of the Scheduled Castes embodied in the Constitution.

Part III—Clause 2

This is not a new demand. It replaces Clause 6 of the Poona Pact which provides that the system of representation for the Scheduled Castes by reserved seats shall continue until determined by mutual consent between the communities concerned in the settlement. Since there is no safe method of ascertaining the will of the Scheduled Castes as to how to amend and alter the safeguards provided for them it is necessary to formulate a plan which will take the place of Clause 6 of the Pact. Provisions having similar objectives to those contained in the proposal exist in the Constitution of Australia, America and South Africa.

In dealing with a matter of this sort two considerations have to be borne in mind. One is that it is not desirable to rule out the possibility of a change in the safeguards being made in the future by the parties concerned. On the other hand it is by no means desirable to incessant struggle over their revision. If the new Union and State Legislatures are to address themselves successfully to their responsibilities set out in the preamble it is desirable that they should not be distracted by the acute contentions between religions and classes which questions of change in the safeguards are bound to raise. Hence a period of twenty-five years has been laid down before any change could be considered.

Article II, Section II, Part IV

The object of this provision is to see that whatever safeguards are provided for the Scheduled Castes in British India are also provided for the Scheduled Castes in the Indian States. The provision lays down that an Indian State seeking admission to the Union shall have to satisfy that its Constitution contains these safeguards.

Article II—Interpretation

Whether the Scheduled Castes are a minority or not has become a matter of controversy. The purpose of First Provision to set this controversy at rest. The Scheduled Castes are in a worst position as compared to any other minority in India. As such they require and deserve much more protection than any other minority does. The least one can do is to treat them as a minority.

The purpose of Second Provision is to remove the provincial bar. There is no reason why a person who belongs to Scheduled Castes in one Province should lose the benefit of political privileges given by the Constitution merely because he happens to change his domicile.

Appendix II

TEXT OF THE POONA PACT

(1) There shall be seats reserved for the Depressed Classes out of the general electorates seats in the Provincial Legislatures as follows :—

Madras	...	...	...	...	30
Bombay with Sind		...	...	...	15
Punjab	...	...	...	...	8
Bihar and Orissa		...	...	...	18
Central Provinces		...	...	...	20
Assam ...	...	...	...	...	7
Bengal ...	...	...	...	...	30
United Provinces		...	...	...	20
			Total	...	148

These figures are based on the total strength of the Provincial Councils, announced in the Prime Minister's decision.

(2) Election to these seats shall be by joint electorates, subject however, to the following procedure :—

All the members of the Depressed Classes registered in the general electoral roll in a constituency will form an electoral college, which will elect a panel of four candidates belonging to the Depressed Classes for each of such reserved seats, by the method of the single vote; the four getting the highest number of votes in such primary election, shall be candidates for election by the general electorate.

(3) Representation of the Depressed Classes in the Central Legislature shall likewise be on the principle of joint electorates and reserved seats by the method of primary election in the manner provided for in clause (2) above, for their representation in the Provincial Legislatures.

(4) In the Central Legislature, eighteen per cent. of the seats allotted to the general electorate for British India in the said Legislature shall be reserved for the Depressed Classes.

(5) The system of primary election to a panel of candidates for election to the Central and Provincial Legislatures, as hereinbefore mentioned, shall come to an end after the first ten years, unless terminated sooner by mutual agreement under the provision of clause (6) below.

(6) The system of representation of the Depressed Classes by reserved seats in the Provincial and Central Legislatures as provided for in clauses (1) and (4) shall continue until determined by mutual agreement between the communities concerned in the settlement.

(7) Franchise for the Central and Provincial Legislatures for the Depressed Classes shall be as indicated in the Lothian Committee Report.

(8) There shall be no disabilities attaching to anyone on the ground of his being a member of the Depressed Class in regard to any elections to local bodies or appointment to the Public Services. Every endeavour shall be made to secure fair representation of the Depressed Classes in these respects, subject to such educational qualifications as may be laid down for appointment to the Public Services.

(9) In every Province out of the educational grant an adequate sum shall be earmarked for providing educational facilities to the Members of the Depressed Classes.

Appendix III

DISADVANTAGES OF THE POONA PACT

1. The Poona Pact was intended to devise a method whereby the Scheduled Castes would be able to return to the Legislature representatives of their choice. This intention has been completely nullified as will be seen from the following series of statistics. The series have been constructed from the results of the last elections which took place in February 1946.

2. The statistical data is arranged in four series of tables :—

First Series show the votes secured by the successful Caste Hindu candidate and the successful Scheduled Caste candidate in the final election.

Second Series show in how many cases did reliance on reservation clause become necessary for the success of the Scheduled Caste candidate in the final election and in how many he succeeded without the benefit of reservation.

Third Series show the relative voting strength of the Caste Hindus and the Scheduled Castes in constituencies in which seats are reserved for the Scheduled Castes.

Fourth Series show the position in the primary election of the Scheduled Caste candidates who became successful in the final elections.

3. The conclusions that follow from these figures will not escape those who care to examine them. The figures prove the following propositions :—

(i) That every of the Scheduled Caste candidate who became successful in the final election owed his success to the votes of the caste Hindus and not of the Scheduled Castes. A great many of them came to the top of the poll and secured votes equal to and in some cases larger than those obtained by Caste Hindu candidates (see Tables in the First Series). Secondly, in very few constituencies was the successful Scheduled Caste candidate required to rely on reservation (see Tables in the Second Series). This is a most unexpected phenomenon. Anyone who compares the voting strength of the Scheduled Castes with the voting strength of the Caste Hindus in the different constituencies (see Tables in the Third Series) would realize that the voting strength of the Scheduled Castes is so small that such a phenomenon could never have occurred if only the Scheduled Caste voters had voted for the Scheduled

Caste candidates. That they have occurred is proof positive that the success of the Scheduled Caste candidates in the final election is conditioned by the Caste Hindu votes.

(ii) That comparing the results of the Primary election with those of the Final election (see Tables in the Fourth Series) the Scheduled Caste candidate who was elected in the Final election was one who had failed in the Primary election (if the Primary election be treated as a final election and the constituency be treated as a single-member constituency).

(iii) Owing to the extreme disparity between the voting strength of the Hindus and the Scheduled Castes—disparity which will not disappear even under adult suffrage—a system of joint electorates will not succeed in giving the Scheduled Castes the chance of returning their true representatives.

(iv) The Poona Pact has completely disfranchised the Scheduled Castes in as much as candidates whom they rejected in the Primary elections—which is a true index of their will—have been returned in the Final election by the votes of the Caste Hindus.

The Poona Pact is thus fraught with mischief. It was accepted because of the coercive fast of Mr. Gandhi and because of the assurance given at the time that the Hindus will not interfere in the election of the Scheduled Castes.

FIRST SERIES

Votes obtained by the successful Scheduled Caste candidates as compared with the votes secured by the successful Caste Hindu candidates.

		Page No.
Part I.	Madras	58
Part II.	Bengal	59
Part III.	Bombay	60
Part IV.	U. P.	61
Part V.	C. P.	62
Part VI.	Assam	63
Part VII.	Orissa	63

First Series

I. MADRAS

Name of the Constituency.	Seats.	Votes polled by successful Hindu candidates.	Votes polled by successful Scheduled Caste candidates.
1. Coconada	2	32,607	28,544
2. Ellore	2	37,618	38,195
3. Bandar	2	69,319	70,931
4. Ongole	2	50,906	49,992
5. Penukonda	2	17,406	18,125
6. Kurnool	2	32,756	32,294
7. Chingleput	2	13,865	15,129
8. Thiruvalur	2	17,225	17,818
9. Ranipet	2	21,249	21,059
10. Tiruvannamalai	2	31,476	32,132
11. Tindivanam	2	25,626	25,442
12. Chidambaram	2	15,272	14,874
13. Tanjore	2	26,904	16,133
14. Mannargudi	2	29,932	30,116
15. Ariyalur	2	22,656	20,520
16. Sattur	2	30,988	29,530
17. Malapuram	2	28,229	28,085
18. Namakkal	2	15,433	15,085

First Series

II. BENGAL

Name of the Constituency.	Seats.	Votes polled by successful Hindu candidates.	Votes polled by successful Scheduled Caste candidates.	
1. Burdwan Central	2	42,858	33,903	—
2. Burdwan, North-West	2	32,270	25,723	—
3. Birbhum	2	24,629	20,252	—
4. Bankura, West	2	30,388	21,266	—
5. Thurgram-cum-Ghatal	2	40,900	19,060	—
6. Hooghly, North-East	2	26,132	18,768	—
7. Howrah	2	40,608	36,099	—
8. 24 Parganas, South-East	2	50,345	38,459	—
9. 24 Parganas, North-West	2	45,339	48,272	—
10. Nadia	2	30,489	28,054	—
11. Murshidabad	2	32,386	26,958	—
12. Jessore	2	38,665	41,434	—
13. Khulna	3	79,218	57,724	44,043
14. Malda	2	32,728	12,796	—
15. Dinajpur	3	46,146	35,127	30,839
16. Jalpaiguri-cum-Siliguri	3	30,950	26,109	13,829
17. Rangpur	3	46,869	29,657	23,237
18. Bogra-cum-Pabna	2	43,249	31,515	—
19. Dacca, East	2	51,808	31,392	—
20. Mymensingh, West	2	37,983	32,782	—
21. Mymensingh, East	2	43,678	32,207	—
22. Faridpur	2	70,115	51,450	29,503
23. Bakargunj	2	48,560	28,560	—
24. Tippera	2	60,146	59,051	—

First Series

III. BOMBAY

Name of the Constituency.	Seats.	Votes secured by successful Hindu candidates.			Votes secured by successful Scheduled Caste candidates.
1. Bombay City (Suburban)	3	57,182	47,835	—	59,646
2. Bombay City (Byculla)	3	42,143	41,795	—	43,251
3. Kaira District	4	68,044	63,422	57,394	69,807
4. Surat District	4	40,232	39,985	39,610	39,849
5. Thana, South	3	30,581	27,587	—	11,630
6. Ahmednagar, South	3	25,747	20,948	—	20,908
7. East Khandesh, East	4	38,721	34,349	33,960	36,136
8. Nasik, West	4	37,218	36,794	36,555	42,604
9. Poona, West	3	23,758	23,454	—	24,709
10. Satara, North	4	44,315	42,727	41,474	43,961
11. Sholapur, North-East	3	19,380	16,705	—	18,264
12. Belgaum, North	4	55,787	50,759	49,867	27,682
13. Bijapur, North	3	23,083	20,838	—	16,059
14. Kolaba District	4	41,012	38,864	35,633	17,676
15. Ratnagiri, North	4	13,640	10,985	10,372	11,734

First Series

IV. UNITED PROVINCES

Name of the Constituency.	Seats.	Votes polled by successful Hindu candidates.	Votes polled by successful Scheduled Caste candidates.
1. Lucknow City	2	24,614	14,110
2. Cawnpore City	2	34,550	34,782
3. Agra City	2	17,446	16,343
4. Allahabad City	2	19,870	10,308
5. Badaun District	2	6,716	14,037
6. Jalaun District	2	21,692	15,363
7. Basti District	2	14,450	15,447
8. Almora District	2	36,371	20,605
9. Rai Bareilli	2	15,917	1,889
10. Sitapur District	2	28,665	20,204
11. Gonda District	2	17,949	13,447

First Series

V. CENTRAL PROVINCES

Name of the Constituency.	Seats.	Votes polled by successful Hindu candidates.	Votes polled by successful Scheduled Caste candidates.
1. Nagpur City	2	21,905	23,595
2. Nagpur-Umred	2	8,330	7,847
3. Hinganghat-Wardha	2	11,677	10,781
4. Chanda-Brahmapuri	2	10,208	8,144
5. Chindwara-Sansad	2	16,365	6,190
6. Saugor-Khurai	2	7,829	5,162
7. Raipur	2	8,183	6,112
8. Baloda Bazar	2	21,861	9,659
9. Bilaspur	2	13,109	6,030
10. Mungeli	2	9,600	6,418
11. Tanjgir	2	11,914	7,419
12. Drug	2	5,975	5,593
13. Bhandara-Sakoli	2	16,824	10,491
14. Yeotmal-Daresha	2	10,915	4,719
15. Ellichpur	2	16,298	4,592
16. Chikhli-Mehkar	2	16,397	2,748
17. Akola-Balapur	2	6,455	5,567

First Series

VI. ASSAM

Name of the Constituency.	Seats.	Votes polled by successful Hindu candidates.		Votes polled by successful Scheduled Caste candidates.
1. Kamrup-Saor, South	3	15,890	14,971	13,693
2. Nowgong	1	—	—	14,560
3. Jorhat, North	2	17,429	—	5,809
4. Habibganj	2	10,985	—	9,770
5. Karimganj	2	12,562	—	11,676
6. Silchar	2	17,340	—	7,081

First Series

VII. ORISSA

Name of the Constituency.	Seats.	Votes obtained by successful Hindu candidates.	Votes obtained by successful Scheduled Caste candidates.
1. East Tajpur	2	8,427	8,712
2. East Burgarh	2	4,195	937

SECOND SERIES

NUMBER OF CONSTITUENCIES IN WHICH RESERVATION BECAME NECESSARY FOR THE SCHEDULED CASTE CANDIDATES TO SUCCEED IN ELECTION

Province.	Number of Constituencies in which seats are reserved for the Scheduled Castes.	Number of Constituencies in which there was a conflict	Number of Constituencies in which the contest was due to excess of Hindu candidates.	Number of Constituencies in which the contest was due to excess of Scheduled Caste candidates.	Number of Constituencies in which the contest was due to excess of both.	Number of Constituencies in which reliance on reservation became necessary for the Scheduled Caste candidates to succeed
1. Madras	30	18	14	17	—	None
2. Bengal	30	24	19	24	19	None
3. Bombay	15	15	15	15	15	2
4. C.P.	22	17	14	17	14	2
5. U.P.	15	11	5	11	6	None
6. Assam	—	—	—	—	—	2
7. Orissa	—	2	—	2	—	None
8. Punjab	8	—	—	—	—	—

THIRD SERIES—RELATIVE VOTING STRENGTH OF CASTE HINDUS AND SCHEDULED CASTES

I. MADRAS

Constituency.	Total number of voters in the Constituency.	Total number of Scheduled Caste voters in the Constituency.	Relative proportion of columns 2 and 3.
1	2	3	4
1. Madras City, South—Central ...	26,922	4,082	1: 6.6
2. Chicacole	90,496	8,070	1: 11.2
3. Amalapuram	95,954	28,282	1: 3.4
4. Cocanada	86,932	17,616	1: 4.9
5. Ellore	88,249	16,835	1: 5.24
6. Ongole	110,152	11,233	1: 9.8
7. Gudur	52,415	10,263	1: 5.1
8. Cuddapah	92,572	10,842	1: 8.5
9. Penukonda	74,952	11,896	1: 6.3
10. Bellary	85,928	10,146	1: 8.5
11. Kurnool	72,753	11,679	1: 6.2
12. Tirutanni	77,337	15,243	1: 5.07
13. Chingleput	73,554	22,182	1: 3.3
14. Tiruvallur	81,814	21,287	1: 3.8
15. Ranipet	24,403	11,271	1: 2.1
16. Tiruvannamalai	97,259	15,536	1: 6.2
17. Tindivanam	85,514	19,221	1: 4.4
18. Chidambaram	96,086	16,762	1: 5.7
19. Tirukoyilur	102,482	21,733	1: 4.7
20. Tanjore	99,496	13,198	1: 7.5
21. Mannargudi	69,579	11,547	1: 5.8
22. Ariyalur	113,630	16,772	1: 6.7
23. Palani	92,655	13,521	1: 6.8
24. Sattur	84,169	8,033	1: 10.5
25. Koilpatti	100,521	20,907	1: 4.8
26. Pollachi	63,821	12,808	1: 4.9
27. Namakkal	51,860	11,407	1: 4.5
28. Coondapur	46,032	8,030	1: 5.7
29. Malapuram	70,346	10,808	1: 6.5

THIRD SERIES—RELATIVE VOTING STRENGTH OF CASTE HINDUS AND SCHEDULED CASTES—(*contd.*)

II. BOMBAY

Constituency.	Total number of voters in the Constituency.	Total number of Scheduled Caste voters in the Constituency.	Relative proportion of columns 2 and 3.
1	2	3	4
General Urban.			
1. Bombay City North and Bombay Suburban District	167,002	34,266	1 : 4.8
2. Bombay City—Byculla and Parel ...	152,991	28,520	1 : 5.3
General Rural.			
3. Kaira District	139,508	7,318	1 : 19.06
4. Surat District	85,670	4,765	1 : 18.8
5. Thana, South	67,749	4,668	1 : 14.5
6. Ahmednagar, South	73,162	7,382	1 : 9.9
7. East Khandesh, East	91,377	10,109	1 : 9.35
8. Nasik, West	99,274	12,698	1 : 7.7
9. Poona, West	73,551	13,055	1 : 5.6
10. Satara, North	95,459	11,152	1 : 8.5
11. Sholapur, North-East	64,583	9,713	1 : 6.6
12. Belgaum, North	79,422	18,303	1 : 4.3
13. Bijapur, North	60,655	8,993	1 : 6.7
14. Kolaba District	103,828	5,001	1 : 20.7
15. Ratnagiri, North	32,606	3,529	1 : 9.2

THIRD SERIES—RELATIVE VOTING STRENGTH OF CASTE HINDUS AND SCHEDULED CASTES—(*contd.*)

III. BENGAL

Constituency.	Total number of voters in the Constituency.	Total number of Scheduled Caste voters in the Constituency.	Relative proportion of columns 2 and 3.
1	2	3	4
General Rural.			
1. Burdwan, Central	74,306	24,610	1 : 3.01
2. Burdwan, North-West	80,035	16,830	1 : 4.8
3. Birbhum	103,231	37,637	1 : 2.7
4. Bankura, West	84,128	25,487	1 : 3.3
5. Midnapore, Central	99,961	20,167	1 : 4.95
6. Jhargam-cum-Ghatal	64,031	13,091	1 : 4.85
7. Hooghly, North-East	67,697	20,318	1 : 3.33
8. Howrah	103,346	22,990	1 : 4.5
9. 24 Parganas, South-West	82,366	47,378	1 : 1.7
10. 24 Parganas, North-East	85,477	30,607	1 : 2.78
11. Nadia	90,092	25,605	1 : 3.5
12. Murshidabad	81,083	17,176	1 : 4.8
13. Jessore	121,760	55,052	1 : 2.2
14. Khulna	145,335	76,848	1 : 1.87
15. Malda	73,664	29,010	1 : 2.54
16. Dinajpur	148,804	118,454	1 : 1.25
17. Jalpaiguri-cum-Siliguri	78,552	65,679	1 : 1.2
18. Rangpur	29,437	65,679	1 : 0.44
19. Bogra-cum-Pabna	87,704	33,873	1 : 2.58
20. Dacca, East	94,858	40,238	1 : 2.35
21. Mymensingh, West	98,795	38,046	1 : 2.59
22. Mymensingh, East	68,360	29,588	1 : 2.3
23. Faridpur	172,683	96,319	1 : 1.7
24. Bakarganj, South-West	78,796	49,014	1 : 1.6
25. Tippera	127,097	34,813	1 : 3.61

THIRD SERIES—RELATIVE VOTING STRENGTH OF CASTE HINDUS AND SCHEDULED CASTES—(*contd.*)

IV. UNITED PROVINCES

Constituency.	Total number of voters in the Constituency.	Total number of Scheduled Caste voters in the Constituency.	Relative proportion of columns 2 and 3.
1	2	3	4
General Urban.			
1. Lucknow City	89,412	9,079	1 : 9.8
2. Cawnpore City	131,599	22,515	1 : 5.8
3. Agra City	47,505	10,105	1 : 4.7
4. Allahabad City	55,379	6,854	1 : 8.07
General Rural.			
5. Charanpur District, South-East ...	47,773	7,256	1 : 6 5
6. Bulandshahr District, South-East ...	49,699	7,506	1 : 6.6
7. Agra District, North-East	61,515	8,290	1 : 7.4
8. Manipuri District, North-East ...	51,406	5,878	1 : 8.7
9. Budaun District, East	46,966	7,087	1 : 6.6
10. Jalaun District	68,815	14,611	1 : 4.7
11. Mirzapur District, North	43,648	4,045	1 : 10.7
12. Gorakhpur District, North	43,441	5,626	1 : 7.7
13. Basti District, South	37,084	4,194	1 : 8 8
14. Azamgarh District, West	51,194	8,127	1 : 6.2
15. Almora District	139,217	20,671	1 . 6.7
16. Rae Bareilli District, North-East ...	48,697	10,488	1 : 4 6
17. Sitapur District, North-East ...	76,682	22,913	1 : 3.3
18. Fyzabad District, East	57,154	9,988	1 : 5.7
19. Gonda District, North-East ...	64,225	8,274	1 : 7.7
20. Bara Banki District, North ...	68,285	16,303	1 : 4.18

THIRD SERIES—RELATIVE VOTING STRENGTH OF CASTE HINDUS AND SCHEDULED CASTES—(*contd.*)

V. CENTRAL PROVINCES

Constituency.	Total number of voters in the Constituency.	Total number of Scheduled Caste voters in the Constituency.	Relative proportion of columns 2 and 3.
1	2	3	4
General Urban.			
1. Nagpur City	72,329	14,388	1: 5 02
General Rural.			
2. Nagpur-Umrer	29,267	6,037	1: 4.8
3. Hinghanghat-Wardha	35,201	4,011	1: 9.02
4. Chanda-Brahmapuri	30,132	5,229	1: 5.7
5. Chindwara-Sausar	37,942	3,914	1: 9.7
6. Jubbulpore-Patan	20,587	1,186	1: 17.5
7. Saugor-Khurai	30,660	5,224	1: 5.8
8. Damoh-Hatta	33,284	3,608	1: 9.2
9. Narsinghpur-Gadarwara	35,781	2,019	1: 17.6
10. Raipur	33,053	11,041	1: 2.9
11. Baloda Bazar	46,943	15,636	1: 3.06
12. Bilaspur	33,260	10,547	1: 3.1
13. Mungeli	28,028	10,067	1: 2.7
14. Janjgir	42,763	13,558	1: 3.15
15. Drug	34,883	8,942	1: 3.19
16. Bhandara-Sakoli	47,047	10,399	1: 4.5
17. Ellichpur-Dartapur-Nelghat ...	30,094	2,885	1: 13.8
18. Akola-Belapur	25,912	3,233	1: 8.91
19. Yeotmal-Darwha	20,327	2,020	1: 10.06
20. Chikhli-Mehkar	37,936	3,468	1: 10.9

THIRD SERIES—RELATIVE VOTING STRENGTH OF CASTE HINDUS AND SCHEDULED CASTES—(*contd.*)

VI. BIHAR

Constituency.	Total number of voters in the Constituency.	Total number of Scheduled Caste voters in the Constituency.	Relative proportion of columns 2 and 3.
1	2	3	4
1. East Bihar	35,631	4,618	1: 7.7
2. South Gaya	49,363	10,360	1: 4.7
3. Nawada	41,432	7,684	1: 5.3
4. East Central Shahabad	41,707	5,984	1: 6.9
5. West Gopalganj	33,395	3,415	1: 9.7
6. North Bettiah	25,760	2 831	1: 9.09
7. East Muzaffarpur-Sadr	27,271	3,133	1: 8.7
8. Darbhanga Sadr	26,864	2,116	1: 12.6
9. South-East Samastipur	37,291	2,672	1: 13.9
10. South Sadr-Monghyr	54,229	6,465	1: 8.5
11. Madhipura	26,523	1,284	1: 20.6
12. South-West Purnea	44,232	2,938	1: 15.05
13. Giridih-cum-Ghatra	55,246	4,667	1: 11.8
14. North-East Palamau	23,072	4,237	1: 5.3
15. Central Manbhum	39,626	5,617	1: 7.05

THIRD SERIES—RELATIVE VOTING STRENGTH OF CASTE HINDUS AND SCHEDULED CASTES—(*contd.*)

VII. ASSAM

Constituency.	Total number of voters in the Constituency.	Total number of Scheduled Caste voters in the Constituency.	Relative proportion of columns 2 and 3.
1	2	3	4
1. Nowgong, North-East	26,618	3,569	1 : 7.2
2. Kamrup Sadr, South	33,234	2,117	1 : 15.6
3. Silchar	38,647	4,201	1 : 9.2
4. Karimganj, East	25,701	10,132	1 : 2.5
5. Jorhat, North	26 733	1,360	1 : 19.6
6. Junamganj	39,045	11,603	1 : 3.3
7. Habibganj, North	31,511	9,996	1 : 3.1

THIRD SERIES—RELATIVE VOTING STRENGTH OF CASTE HINDUS AND SCHEDULED CASTES— (*concld.*)

VIII. PUNJAB

Constituency.	Total number of voters in the Constituency.	Total number of Scheduled Caste voters in the Constituency.	Relative proportion of columns 2 and 3.
1	2	3	4
1. South-East Gurgaon	37,815	6,049	1 : 6.2
2. Karnal, North	31,967	5,120	1 : 6.2
3. Ambala and Simla	47,403	17,507	1 : 3.27
4. Hoshiarpur, West	51.084	7,281	1 : 7.0
5. Jullundur	36,570	20,521	1 : 1.8
6. Ludhiana and Ferozepure	52,009	27,354	1 : 1.8
7. Amritsar and Sialkot	38,046	10,328	1 : 3.68
8. Lyallpur and Jhang	32,703	7,602	1 : 4.2

FOURTH SERIES—COMPARISON OF PRIMARY ELECTION AND FINAL ELECTION

I. MADRAS

Constituency.	Scheduled Caste candidate who was successful in final election.			His rank among candidates who fought the general election.	His position in the Primary election treating the Constituency as a single member Constituency.	Votes obtained in the Primary election.	What his success in Primary election due to bare or absolute majority or split vote.
	His Name	His Party Affiliation.	Number of votes secured.				
1. Amalapuram	Pandu Lakshmanaswami	Congress	48,524	1st among 3 ...	3rd (failed) ...	2,683	—
2. Cocanada ...	B S. Murthy ...	Congress	28,544	2nd among 4 (beating 2 Hindus) ..	4th (failed) ...	1,411	—
3. Bandar	Vemula Kurmayya..	Congress	70,931	1st among 6 (beating 4 Hindus) ...	2nd (failed) ...	4,914	—
4. Cuddapah ...	Swarna Nagayya ...	Congress	—	—	1st	3,482	Absolute majority.
5. Penukonda ...	D. Kadrippa ...	Congress	18,125	1st among 4 (beating 1 Hindu and 2 Sch. Castes) ..	1st	2,564	Bare majority.
6. Tiruvannamali ...	R. Thangavelu ...	Congress	32,132	1st among 5 (beating 2 Hindus and 2 Sch. Castes)	1st	1,960	Bare majority.
7. Tindivanam ..	K. Kulashekardas ...	Congress	25,442	2nd among 4 (beating 2 Hindus) ..	1st	2,785	Split vote.
8. Mannargudi ...	Thiagoo Voikarar ...	Congress	30,116	1st among 5 (beating 5 Hindus) ..	1st	2,895	Split vote.
9. Pollachi	C. Krishna Kudumban. ...	Congress	—	—	1st	2,430	Absolute majority.
10. Namakkal ...	M. P. Periyaswami ...	Congress	15,085	2nd among 5 (beating 2 Hindus and 1 Sch. Caste) ...	1st	2,355	Bare majority.

FOURTH SERIES—COMPARISON OF PRIMARY ELECTION AND FINAL ELECTION—(*contd.*)

II. BOMBAY

Constituency.	Scheduled Caste candidate who was successful in final election.			His rank among candidates who fought the general election.	His position in the Primary election treating the Constituency as a single member Constituency.	Votes obtained in the Primary election.	Was his success in Primary election due to bare or absolute majority or split vote.
	His Name.	His Party Affiliation.	Number of votes secured.				
1. Bombay City, North.	Savlaram Gundaji Songaoker.	Congress	59,646	1st among 3 (standing above 2 Hindus) ..	2nd (failed) ..	2,038	—
2. Bombay City, Byculla and Parel.	N. S. Kajrolkar ...	Congress	43,251	1st among 3 (standing above 2 general candidates) ...	2nd (failed) ...	2,098	—
3. East Khandesh, East.	Hiralal Kalyani ...	Congress	36,136	2nd among 4 (beating 2) ..	2nd (failed) ...	1,147	—

FOURTH SERIES—COMPARISON OF PRIMARY ELECTION AND FINAL ELECTION—(*contd.*)

III. CENTRAL PROVINCES

Constituency.	Scheduled Caste candidate who was successful in final election.			His rank among candidates who fought the general election.	His position in the Primary election treating the Constituency as a single member Constituency.	Votes obtained in the Primary election.	Was his success in Primary election due to bare or absolute majority or split vote.
	His Name.	His Party Affiliation.	Number of votes secured.				
1. Nagpur-Umrer ...	Lelendra Ramchandra.	Congress	7,847	2nd	3rd (failed) ...	112	—
2. Hinghanghat-Wardha.	Shanker Vithal ...	Congress	10,781	2nd	4th (failed) ...	56	—
3. Bhandara-Sakoli...	Harnuji Isram ...	Congress	10,491	2nd	3rd (failed) ..	471	—
4. Yeotmal-Darwha.	Daulat-Luxman ...	Congress	4,719	2nd	3rd (failed) ...	126	—

FOURTH SERIES—COMPARISON OF PRIMARY ELECTION AND FINAL ELECTION—(*contd.*)

IV. UNITED PROVINCES

Constituency.	Scheduled Caste candidate who was successful in final election.			His rank among candidates who fought the general election.	His position in the Primary election treating the Constituency as a single member Constituency.	Votes obtained in the Primary election.	Was his success in Primary election due to bare or absolute majority or split vote.
	His Name.	His Party Affiliation.	Number of votes secured.				
1. Agra City ..	Ram Chand	Congress	16,343	2nd	1st	836	Bare majority and split vote.
2. Allahabad City ..	Masuria Din ...	Congress	10,308	2nd	1st	1,701	Bare majority and split vote.
3. Almora	Khushi Ram ...	Congress	20,605	2nd	2nd (failed) ...	937	—

FOURTH SERIES—COMPARISON OF PRIMARY ELECTION AND FINAL ELECTION—(*concld.*)

V. PUNJAB

Constituency.	Scheduled Caste candidate who was successful in final election.			His rank among candidates who fought the general election.	His position in the Primary election treating the Constituency as a single member Constituency.	Votes obtained in the Primary election.	Was his success in Primary election due to bare or absolute majority or split vote.
	His Name.	His Party Affiliation.	Number of votes secured.				
1. South-East Gurgaon.	Prem Singh	Unionist	7,706	2nd	1st	1,353	Split vote.
2. Karnal, North ...	Sunder	Congress	3,136	2nd	1st	519	Bare majority.
3. Ambala-Simla ...	Prithvi Singh Azad...	Congress	10,503	2nd	3rd (failed) ...	1,392	—
4. Hoshiyarpur, West.	Mehr Chand ...	Congress	16,307	2nd	3rd (failed) ...	641	—
5. Jullundur ...	Gurbanta Singh .	Congress	21,476	1st .. .	1st	—	—
6. Ludhyana-Ferozpur.	Matu Ram	Congress	24,352	1st	4th (failed) ...	812	—
7. Lyallpur and Jhang.	Harbhaj Ram ...	—	8,312	2nd	2nd (failed) ..	1,166	—

Appendix IV

STATISTICS OF POPULATION

The population of the Scheduled Caste in 1941 is estimated at 48,793,180. Can this figure be accepted as accurate ?

In coming to a definite conclusion on this issue the following points must be borne in mind :—

(i) The population of the Scheduled Castes in 1941 as compared with their population in 1931 shows a decline.

(ii) The population of all other communities during the same period shows an increase of 15 p. c.

The question is whether there is any special reason why the population of the Scheduled Castes should have declined.

Was the basis for computation of the population of the Scheduled Castes in 1931 the same as in 1941 ? The answer is in the affirmative. The figures given for 1931 are the result of recasting of the Census of 1931 in the light of the definition of "Untouchables" given by the Lothian Committee. The same basis was adopted in 1941. It cannot therefore be said that the decline in the population of the Scheduled Castes in 1941 was due to an over-estimate made in 1931.

It is true that the Census for 1941 does not give any figures for the Scheduled Castes for Ajmer-Merwara and Gwalior State. But even adding to the total for 1941 the figures for these two areas as they stood in 1931 the population comes to only 49,538,145 which still shows a comparative decline.

The want of any proper explanation for the decline of the Scheduled Caste population and an increase in the population of all other communities during the same decade only re-inforces the impression which every honest student of Indian census has formed namely that the Census of India has over a number of decades ceased to be an operation in demography. It has become a political affair. Every community seems to be attempting to artificially augment its numbers at the cost of some other community for the sake of capturing greater and greater degree of political power in its own hands. The Scheduled Castes seem to have been made a common victim for the satisfaction of the combined greed of the other communities who through their propagandists or enumerators are able to control the operations and the results of the Census.

In the light of these circumstances it is fair to demand that an accurate figure for the population of the Scheduled Castes would be the Census figure as corrected by the inclusion of the population for Ajmer-Merwara and Gwalior State *plus* an increase of 15 per cent. to give them the benefit of the general rise in the population.

APPENDIX IV

POPULATION FIGURES

TABLE I

POPULATION OF DIFFERENT COMMUNITIES ACCORDING TO THE CENSUS OF 1941

	Hindus.	Scheduled Castes.	Muslims.	Sikhs.	Indian Christians.	Anglo-Indians.	Parsis.
Provinces	150,890,146	39,920,807	79,398,503	4,165,097	3,245,706	113,936	101,968
Ajmer-Merwara	376,481	?	89,899	867	3,895	1,005	
Assam*	3,586,932	676,291	3,442,479	3,464	37,750	634	2
Baluchistan	39,521	5,102	438,930	11,918	2,633	263	75
Bengal	17,680,054	7,378,970	33,005,434	16,281	110,923	31,619	86,270
Bihar	22,173,890	4,340,379	4,716,314	13,213	24,693	5,963	547
Orissa	5,594,535	1,238,171	146,301	232	26,584	789	13
Bombay	14,700,242	1,855,148	1,920,368	6,044	338,812	14,034	43,467
Sind	1,038,292	191,634	3,208,325	31,011	13,232	2,731	1,936
Central Provinces and Berar	9,880,583	3,051,413	783,697	14,996	48,260	4,538	2,014
Coorg	105,013	25,740	14,730	*Nil*	3,309	80	12
Delhi	444,532	122,693	304,971	16,157	10,494	3,408	284
Madras	34,731,330	8,068,492	3,896,452	418	2,001,082	28,661	369
N.W.F.P.	180,321	?	2,788,797	57,939	5,426	837	24
Punjab	6,301,737	1,248,635	16,217,242	3,757,401	486,038	5,891	4,327
United States	34,094,511	11,717,158	8,416,308	232,445	131,327	13,383	1,375
States and Agencies	55,227,180	8,892,373	12,659,593	1,526,350	2,794,959	26,468	12,922
INDIA	206,117,326	48,813,180	92,058,096	5,691,447	6,040,665	140,422	114,490

* Tribes 6,484,996.

TRIBES

Provinces	16,713,256
States and Agencies	8,728,233
INDIA	25,441,489

TABLE II

VARIATION IN POPULATION BY COMMUNITIES

	1931			1941			Increase + Decrease —
	Provinces	States and Agencies	Total India	Provinces	States and Agencies	Total India	Total Percentage
Hindus	139,319,979	50,335,391	189,654,370	150,890,146	55,227,180	206,117,326	+ 26,462,956
Scheduled Castes	38,409,009	11,131,761	49,540,770	39,920,807	8,892,373	48,793,180	— 747,590
Muslims	67,020,443	10,657,102	77,677,545	79,398,503	12,659,598	92,058,096	+ 14,381,551
Sikhs	3,220,997	1,114,774	4,335,771	4,165,097	1,526,350	5,691,447	+ 1,355,676
Christians	3,866,660	2,430,103	6,296,763	3,471,430	2,834,119	6,316,549	+ 19,786
Parsis	96,549	13,203	109,752	101,968	12,922	114,890	+ 5,138